ANCIENT ROME

MIKE CORBISHLEY

THIRD EDITION

CHELSEA HOUSE
PUBLISHERS

An imprint of Infobase Publishing

Cultural Atlas for Young People
ANCIENT ROME
Third Edition

Copyright © 2007 The Brown Reference Group plc

Chelsea House
An imprint of Infobase Publishing
132 West 31st Street
New York, NY 10001

Library of Congress Cataloging-in-Publication Data
available upon request.

ISBN: 0-8160-6822-4

ISBN 13 digit: 978-0-8160-6822-7

Set ISBN: 978-0-8160-7218-7

Chelsea House books are available at special discounts when purchased in bulk quantities for businesses, associations, institutions, or sales promotions. Please call our Special Sales Department in New York at (212) 967-8800 or (800) 322-8755.

You can find Chelsea House on the World Wide Web at:
http://www.chelseahouse.com

The Brown Reference Group
(incorporating Andromeda Oxford Limited)
8 Chapel Place, Rivington Street
London EC2A 3DQ
www.brownreference.com

For The Brown Reference Group plc:
Editorial Director: Lindsey Lowe
Project Editor: Graham Bateman
Editor: Virginia Carter
Design: Steve McCurdy
Senior Managing Editor: Tim Cooke

Printed in Singapore
10 9 8 7 6 5 4 3 2 1

Artwork and Picture Credits

Maps drawn by Lovell Johns, Oxford; Alan Mais, Hornchurch; Location Map Services, Fleet; Thames Cartographic Services, Maidenhead. All site plans by John Brennan, Oxford.
Color artwork by Kevin Maddison and Chris Forsey; other artwork by Peter Chesterton.
Key: t = top, c = center, b = bottom, l = left, r = right

Title page Robert Harding Associates. 5 ZEFA. 8/9 Mauro Pucciarelli, Rome. 10bl Mauro Pucciarelli, Rome. 12 Scala, Florence. 13l Leonard von Matt. 13r Conrad Helbig, Zefa. 14tr Archivo Iconografico, S.A./CORBIS. 14cr Alinari. 15 Giraudon. 16 Scala, Florence. 17 Clive Spong. 18tr German Archaeological Institute, Rome. 21tr Mauro Pucciarelli, Rome. 24t German Archaeological Institute, Rome. 24bl Sonia Halliday, Weston Turville. 25tl Mario Gerardi Rome. 25tr Ray Gardner, London. 25b Mario Gerardi, Rome. 26tl, 26tr, 26cr Ilse Schneider-Lengyel, Phaidon Archive, Oxford. 26bl Alan Hutchison Library, London. 26/27 Alinari. 27t Leonard von Matt. 27c Alinari. 28/29 Roger Ressmeyer/CORBIS. 29t Malcolm Smythe. 29r Ronald Sheridan, London. 30 Araldo de Luca/ CORBIS. 31 Mauro Pucciarelli, Rome. 32l John Fuller, Cambridge. 32r Mario Gerardi, Rome. 34l Jean Roubier, Paris. 34r Bernard and Catherine Desjeux/CORBIS. 36bl Hirmer Fotoarchiv, Munich. 36tr Alinari. 36cr Ray Gardner. 36br German Archaeological Institute, Rome. 37t Ray Gardner. 37b Scala. 38tr Michael Holford. 38cr Scala, Florence. 38bl Ronald Sheridan, London. 38/39 Louvre, Paris. 39t Royal Commission on Historical Monuments. 39c A.A.M. van der Heyden, Amsterdam. 41r Michael Holford, Loughton. 42l Mario Gerardi, Rome. 44l Roger Wood, London. 44r Museo della Civilta Romana. 46b, 46t Michael Dixon, Dover. 47 Michael Vickers, Oxford. 48/49 Hayward Art Group. 50/51 Sheridan Photo Library. 52t Brian Brake, John Hillelson Agency, London. 52br Bernard Regent, Alan Hutchison Library, London. 53t, 53b Sonia Halliday, Weston Turville. 54t Michael Vickers, Oxford. 54b Roger Wood, London. 55t Elsevier Archive, Amsterdam. 55b Alan Hutchison Library, London. 56 Brian Brake, John Hillelson Agency, London. 57 Scala, Florence. 60cl Michael Holford. 60cr Rheinisches Landesmuseum, Trier. 60bl Klaus Kerth, Zefa. 62t Roger Agache, Service des Fouilles, Abbeville. 62b Dick Barnard, Milverton. 63tr Archivo Iconografico, S.A./CORBIS. 63cl Heberden Coin Room, Ashmolean Museum, Oxford. 63cr Michael S. Yamashita/CORBIS. 63bl Paul Almasay/CORBIS. 63br Rheinisches Landesmuseum, Trier. 64t A.F. Kersting, London. 65 Dick Barnard, Milverton, Somerset. 66t British Museum, London. 66b Michael Holford. 68/69 Brian Brake, John Hillelson Agency, London. 70 Paul Hignam/English Heritage. 71t Sussex Archaeological Society. 71b Sunday Times, London. 72t Scala. 72b Michael Holford. 75 Lothar Beckel, Bad Ischl, Austria. 76t Michael Dixon. 76bl Sonia Halliday, Weston Turville. 76br Nikos Kontos, Athens. 78tr Photoresources, Dover. 78bl Ronald Sheridan, London. 78br Richard T. Nowitz/CORBIS. 79l Graham Speake, Oxford. 80bl Michael Dixon, Dover. 82tr W. Wilkinson, London. 82cl Michael Dixon, Dover. 82bl Sonia Halliday, Weston Turville. 83 Davil Brill, © National Geographic Society. 84bl Rouen Museum. 84br Robert Harding Associates, London. 86t Ronald Sheridan, London. 86c R.D. Wilkinson, London. 86b Mrs Seton Lloyd, reproduced from J.B. Segal, *Edessa the Blessed City* by permission of Thames & Hudson. 87 Research Collections, Princeton University. 88 Sonia Halliday, Weston Turville. 89bl W. Brann, Zefa. 89r Sonia Halliday, Weston Turville. 90b Florence Archaeological Museum (Photoresources). 90/91 Leonard von Matt, Buochs.

Contents

Introduction

This book is about the Romans. It will help you step back 2,000 years and look at their world. The Romans were renowned for their buildings and feats of engineering. Nowadays we have motor-powered machinery to do most of the construction work for us. The Romans did invent machinery and were able to survey and draw accurate plans. However, we can still wonder at their determination to build, for example, a race track for chariots that was 650 yards (590 m) long and could hold 350,000 spectators (Rome's Circus Maximus).

Writing and literature were introduced into all of the regions that became part of their empire. The Latin language was soon being used throughout the Roman world. People used it for business and for legal transactions. They were also able to enjoy plays at the theater and books, including stories, histories, and poems. A great deal of Roman literature has survived because it was copied by monks in the Middle Ages from ancient originals.

An important difference between the Roman Empire and most countries today is the large number of nations who lived there. There were about 60 million people living in the Roman Empire, at its biggest. They were people who had been brought into the Roman world, often by conquest. These "new" Romans usually thought of themselves as Roman—certainly they were encouraged to do so and to learn to use the standard language, Latin.

In many ways it could be said that the Roman state was founded on slavery. There were large numbers of slaves owned throughout the empire who were made to work on farms, in industries, and in homes. Many of them were treated badly, but most of them were well cared for by their masters and mistresses.

The Roman world was large, and it covered a very long period of history. The Romans taught their children that the city of Rome had been founded in 753 B.C.E.; their empire in the West was taken over by German armies in 476 C.E. So Rome and a Roman way of life were important for more than 1,000 years.

Ancient Rome is divided into two main sections. The first, **The History of an Empire**, builds up the story of the Romans and tells how they gradually became the most important power in the world. Throughout this section there are maps illustrating specific themes or topics in the main text. Many of these maps are accompanied by charts giving important dates and events in Roman history. The second part, **The Geography of an Empire**, looks at the effect the Romans had on the lands they took over. The maps in this section are more typically atlaslike, containing details of rivers, towns, roads, mountains, and lowlands. Important Roman towns and villages, with their modern and Latin names, can be located using the Gazetteer on pages 93–94.

The book is called an atlas—and that is what it is. It is full of maps to help you understand the story and to see where places and events were. You might like to compare these maps with those in a modern atlas to see how things have changed. Our story is arranged in double-page spreads. Each spread is a complete story. So you can read the book from beginning to end, or just dip into it to learn about a specific topic. The Glossary on page 92 contains definitions of historical and Roman terms used in the book.

Abbreviations used in this book
B.C.E. = Before Common Era (also known as B.C.).
C.E. = Common Era (also known as A.D.). c. = *circa* (about).
in = inch; ft = foot; yd = yard; mi = mile.
cm = centimeter; m = meter; km = kilometer.
When referring to dates, early third century B.C.E., for example, means about 220 or 210 B.C.E., and late third century B.C.E. means about 290 or 280 B.C.E.

▶ The Triumphal Arch of Septimius Severus in the Roman Forum.

Timelines

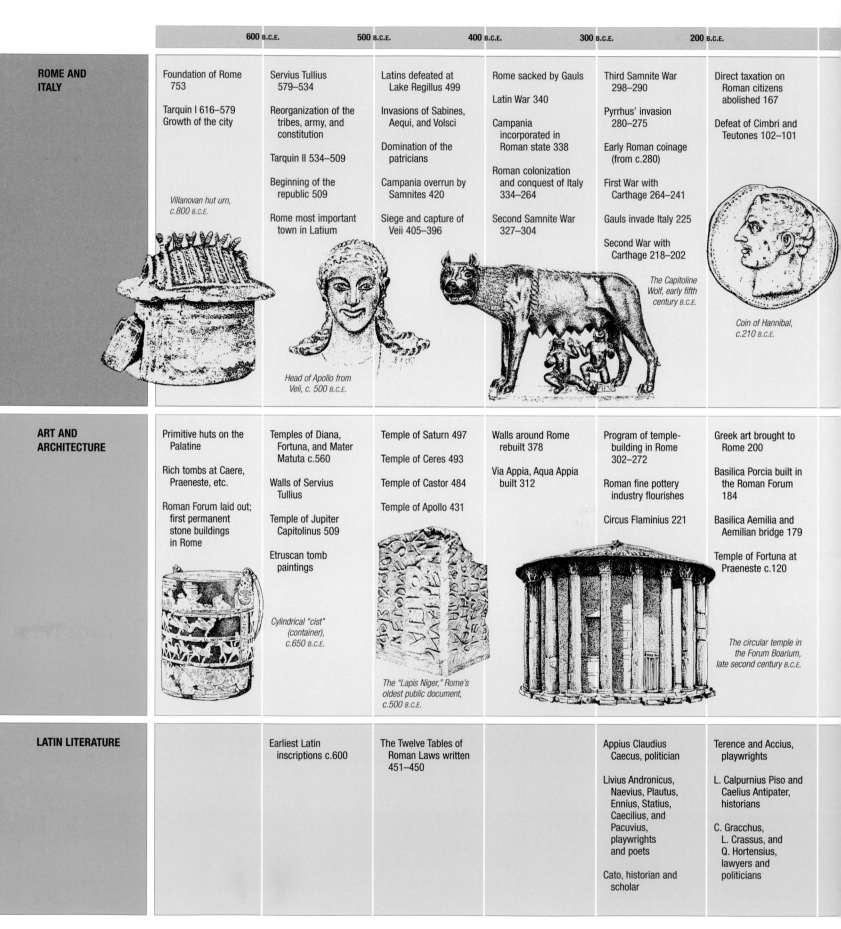

	600 B.C.E.	500 B.C.E.	400 B.C.E.	300 B.C.E.	200 B.C.E.
ROME AND ITALY	Foundation of Rome 753 Tarquin I 616–579 Growth of the city *Villanovan hut urn, c.800 B.C.E.*	Servius Tullius 579–534 Reorganization of the tribes, army, and constitution Tarquin II 534–509 Beginning of the republic 509 Rome most important town in Latium *Head of Apollo from Veii, c. 500 B.C.E.*	Latins defeated at Lake Regillus 499 Invasions of Sabines, Aequi, and Volsci Domination of the patricians Campania overrun by Samnites 420 Siege and capture of Veii 405–396	Rome sacked by Gauls Latin War 340 Campania incorporated in Roman state 338 Roman colonization and conquest of Italy 334–264 Second Samnite War 327–304 *The Capitoline Wolf, early fifth century B.C.E.*	Third Samnite War 298–290 Pyrrhus' invasion 280–275 Early Roman coinage (from c.280) First War with Carthage 264–241 Gauls invade Italy 225 Second War with Carthage 218–202	Direct taxation on Roman citizens abolished 167 Defeat of Cimbri and Teutones 102–101 *Coin of Hannibal, c.210 B.C.E.*
ART AND ARCHITECTURE	Primitive huts on the Palatine Rich tombs at Caere, Praeneste, etc. Roman Forum laid out; first permanent stone buildings in Rome *Cylindrical "cist" (container), c.650 B.C.E.*	Temples of Diana, Fortuna, and Mater Matuta c.560 Walls of Servius Tullius Temple of Jupiter Capitolinus 509 Etruscan tomb paintings	Temple of Saturn 497 Temple of Ceres 493 Temple of Castor 484 Temple of Apollo 431 *The "Lapis Niger," Rome's oldest public document, c.500 B.C.E.*	Walls around Rome rebuilt 378 Via Appia, Aqua Appia built 312	Program of temple-building in Rome 302–272 Roman fine pottery industry flourishes Circus Flaminius 221	Greek art brought to Rome 200 Basilica Porcia built in the Roman Forum 184 Basilica Aemilia and Aemilian bridge 179 Temple of Fortuna at Praeneste c.120 *The circular temple in the Forum Boarium, late second century B.C.E.*
LATIN LITERATURE		Earliest Latin inscriptions c.600	The Twelve Tables of Roman Laws written 451–450		Appius Claudius Caecus, politician Livius Andronicus, Naevius, Plautus, Ennius, Statius, Caecilius, and Pacuvius, playwrights and poets Cato, historian and scholar	Terence and Accius, playwrights L. Calpurnius Piso and Caelius Antipater, historians C. Gracchus, L. Crassus, and Q. Hortensius, lawyers and politicians

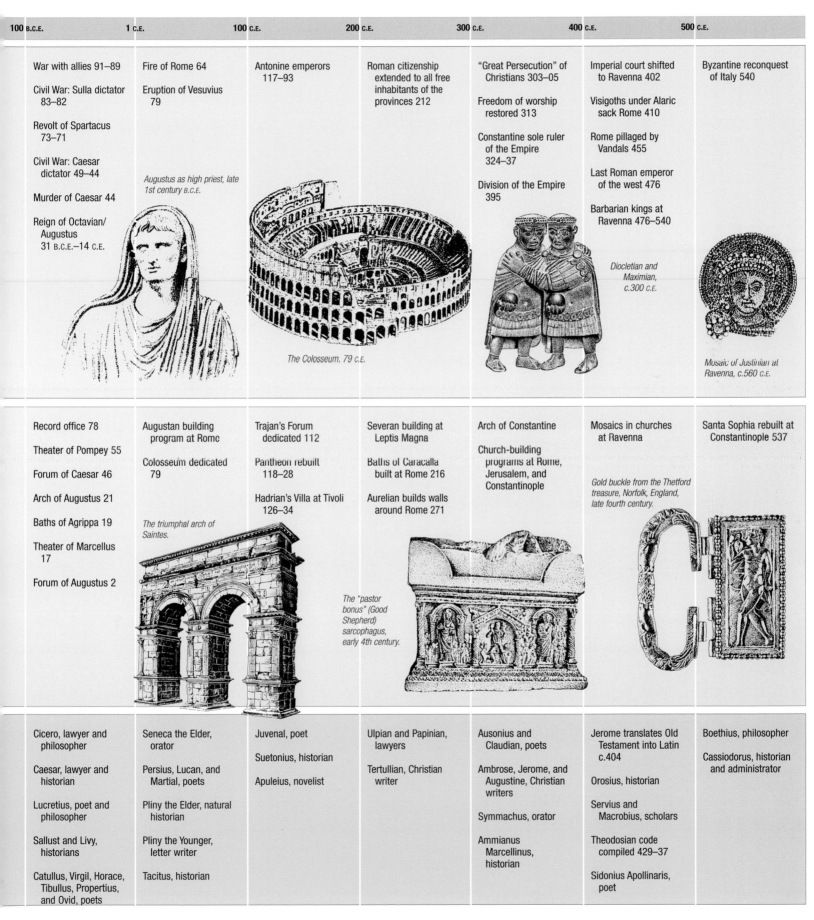

War with allies 91–89

Civil War: Sulla dictator 83–82

Revolt of Spartacus 73–71

Civil War: Caesar dictator 49–44

Murder of Caesar 44

Reign of Octavian/ Augustus 31 B.C.E.–14 C.E.

Fire of Rome 64

Eruption of Vesuvius 79

Augustus as high priest, late 1st century B.C.E.

Antonine emperors 117–93

The Colosseum, 79 C.E.

Roman citizenship extended to all free inhabitants of the provinces 212

"Great Persecution" of Christians 303–05

Freedom of worship restored 313

Constantine sole ruler of the Empire 324–37

Division of the Empire 395

Diocletian and Maximian, c.300 C.E.

Imperial court shifted to Ravenna 402

Visigoths under Alaric sack Rome 410

Rome pillaged by Vandals 455

Last Roman emperor of the west 476

Barbarian kings at Ravenna 476–540

Byzantine reconquest of Italy 540

Mosaic of Justinian at Ravenna, c.560 C.E.

Record office 78

Theater of Pompey 55

Forum of Caesar 46

Arch of Augustus 21

Baths of Agrippa 19

Theater of Marcellus 17

Forum of Augustus 2

Augustan building program at Rome

Colosseum dedicated 79

The triumphal arch of Saintes.

Trajan's Forum dedicated 112

Pantheon rebuilt 118–28

Hadrian's Villa at Tivoli 126–34

Severan building at Leptis Magna

Baths of Caracalla built at Rome 216

Aurelian builds walls around Rome 271

The "pastor bonus" (Good Shepherd) sarcophagus, early 4th century.

Arch of Constantine

Church-building programs at Rome, Jerusalem, and Constantinople

Mosaics in churches at Ravenna

Gold buckle from the Thetford treasure, Norfolk, England, late fourth century.

Santa Sophia rebuilt at Constantinople 537

Cicero, lawyer and philosopher

Caesar, lawyer and historian

Lucretius, poet and philosopher

Sallust and Livy, historians

Catullus, Virgil, Horace, Tibullus, Propertius, and Ovid, poets

Seneca the Elder, orator

Persius, Lucan, and Martial, poets

Pliny the Elder, natural historian

Pliny the Younger, letter writer

Tacitus, historian

Juvenal, poet

Suetonius, historian

Apuleius, novelist

Ulpian and Papinian, lawyers

Tertullian, Christian writer

Ausonius and Claudian, poets

Ambrose, Jerome, and Augustine, Christian writers

Symmachus, orator

Ammianus Marcellinus, historian

Jerome translates Old Testament into Latin c.404

Orosius, historian

Servius and Macrobius, scholars

Theodosian code compiled 429–37

Sidonius Apollinaris, poet

Boethius, philosopher

Cassiodorus, historian and administrator

Part One

The History of an Empire

▲ Hannibal leading his army across the Alps to attack the Romans in 218 B.C.E.—from a central Italian plate.

▶ Tiber Island, Rome, with the ruins of the Pons Aemilius (second century B.C.E.) in the foreground.

A Land Called Italy

"BEYOND THE FOOTHILL OF THE ALPS you reach the beginning of what is now called Italy," wrote the geographer Strabo in the time of the first emperor, Augustus.

The name Italy comes from the word used by the Romans: Italia. But it is probably even older than that. It may come from a word the Greeks used, *witalia*, meaning "the land of cattle." This book is not just about a "land of cattle" but about a huge empire that stretched from the North Sea to the Black Sea and from the Atlas Mountains in North Africa to the Danube River in central Europe.

Varied landscape

The story of Rome and its empire begins with the land of Italy, a large country made up of different landscapes. A mountain range running north and south, the Apennines, divides the country like a backbone. On the eastern side there is little room between these mountains and the sea. There are few natural harbors, and the soil is poor. The western side has a better climate, with a great deal of land suitable for farming. This was the side most people wanted to settle in.

▼ Monte Corno in the Gran Sasso (the "Great Crag"). At more than 9,000 ft (2,700 m) it dominates the Apennines in central Italy and is the highest point in the peninsula.

Rivers of Italy

The Tiber and the Arno Rivers were very important in the history of the first people who settled in Italy. The plains around the rivers were good farming land, and the rivers themselves were used as main routes inland. The western side of Italy also has more rainfall than the east as well as good harbors.

In northern Italy, south of the Alps, lies an enormous plain with the Po River running for 350 miles (560 km) through it. The river brings down silt that helps make the soil fertile. The marshy land this produced on the coast of the Adriatic Sea was reclaimed during the Roman period by earth walls and drainage canals.

Rich in resources

Italy was much more wooded in early times than it is today. There were forests of larch and maple on the slopes of the Alps, and the area around Rome produced pine and beech. There was always plenty of good stone for building, as well as clay for making bricks and tiles and for pottery.

The farming land was suitable for all sorts of animals, including cattle, sheep, goats, and horses. The Romans grew a variety of crops such as wheat, vegetables, grapes for wine, and olives for eating and for making their oil.

The people of Italy

The people who came to this fertile land were from all over the Mediterranean and beyond. Celtic-speaking Gauls came from beyond the Alps, and Greeks settled on the southern coasts and in Sicily, calling the land Magna Graecia ("Great Greece").

Over the centuries the Romans took over more and more neighboring countries. By the second century C.E. the Romans controlled an empire that included lands from Britain to North Africa, from Spain to Syria, and from Egypt to Germany. Eventually all the peoples in these lands became "Roman." For example, the emperor Diocletian came from the far-off province of Dalmatia (now Croatia and Bosnia), and the poet Martial thought of himself as a Roman even though he was born in what we now call Spain.

▶ Only about one-fifth of Italy is flat plain. The rest is mountainous or hilly. Northern Italy shares its cooler climate with central Europe. The southern climate is hotter and typically Mediterranean.

Feet
6,500
3,250
650
0

△12,792 Mountain peak (feet)
—·—·— International boundar
— — — Regional boundary
■ Capital city

Scale 1:4 250 000

0   150 kr
0   100

The Mysterious Etruscans

CENTURIES BEFORE THE ROMANS, THE area north of Rome, called Etruria, was home to people called the Etruscans. The Romans themselves liked to believe that their country was founded by warrior heroes who were descended from the gods. But some Roman and Greek writers tried to investigate the earlier peoples of the region and were very curious about these Etruscans.

The Etruscan people gradually developed their way of life in this hilly but fertile region of west-central Italy. By the seventh century B.C.E. they had formed themselves into 12 separate states. Each state was like an independent country, with its own capital city, but they were all Etruscan.

Together the Etruscan states began to conquer other territories around them. By the sixth century B.C.E. there were Etruscan cities as far north as Mantua and as far south as Salerno.

A rich and powerful people

The Etruscans became wealthy through agriculture, through trade with the Greeks and other peoples, and because they developed industries such as metalworking and pottery. They built large cities that were laid out with roads and had sewage and water systems.

In fact, many of the ideas we think of as Roman were invented by the Etruscans. For example, the Etruscans developed a system to bring water into their cities by aqueducts. The name for Rome was originally an Etruscan word: Roma.

Lost language

One of the reasons we know far less about the Etruscans than we do about the later Romans is because of their language. There were people still speaking Etruscan in the second century C.E., but the language was lost after that time. Only a few inscriptions survive today.

Most of our recorded information about Etruscan customs and beliefs consists of the statements of Greek and Roman writers who were often prejudiced.

Etruscan tombs and art

We do have plenty of evidence about the Etruscans from the decorated underground tombs built for the rich. The cemeteries were in special areas outside the cities. Skillful architects, builders, and artists were employed to create these tombs.

Below ground the elaborate tombs are built like houses for the dead, complete with furniture. They

◄ Tomb portrait from Tarquinia. Many of the tombs were covered with beautiful wall paintings. From an inscription we know that this lady with an elaborate hairstyle is called Velia.

▼ Major Etruscan cities in the sixth century B.C.E. The Etruscan civilization developed between the Arno and Tiber Rivers west of the Apennines.

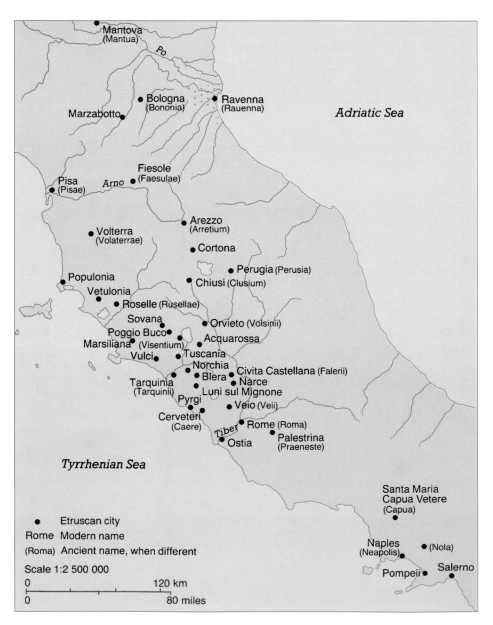

The Etruscans were skilled metalworkers, especially in bronze. This statue of a warrior was one of the objects placed in an underground tomb.

This tomb in Caere shows what part of an Etruscan house would have looked like, including couch, chair, and shields on the walls.

have colorful paintings on the walls, and sometimes on the ceilings as well. The paintings often show the ceremonies that were conducted at a person's funeral, including open-air banquets with dancers, musicians, games, and sports. Above ground the great, tall mounds of earth that mark the tombs often still survive to this day.

The Etruscans believed that there was another life following death. People were buried in ceremonial style, with food for the next world. A large number of objects were also placed in these tombs—jewelry, statues, and vases, for example.

Today these fine Etruscan tombs are still under threat from treasure hunters who break in and steal the fine artwork and sell it overseas at high prices.

The Beginnings of Rome

ALTHOUGH THE ETRUSCANS WERE POWERFUL and conquered territory in central Italy, they were not the only people who lived there. Other tribes were the Samnites, Umbrians, Sabines, and Latins. In the city of Roma—Rome—the Latins were the largest group.

The Latin language

Latin was the language spoken by the Latins who lived in the plain around and to the south of Rome. Latin probably arrived from across the Alps before the eighth century B.C.E.

As the Roman state became bigger, the language spread to millions of people across the Roman world. From there Latin has passed into many European languages. Here are some examples from English with the Latin in brackets: civilian (*civis*, a citizen of a town), mile (*mille passuum*, a thousand paces), family (*familia*), and second (*secundus*).

Romulus, Remus, and early kings

The Romans believed that Romulus, the first ruler (they called him *rex*, or king), founded the city on April 21 in the year 753 B.C.E. Roman children were all told how Romulus and his twin brother Remus were cast adrift in a basket on the Tiber River by the wicked brother of their step-grandfather.

They were saved by a she-wolf who suckled them. They were discovered by the shepherd of the royal flocks and he and his wife raised them. Later the twins went on to found Rome. According to the story, Romulus killed his brother Remus in an argument.

The site of the city had many advantages: a good river crossing, plenty of fresh water, and pleasant surrounding hills. Years later a writer described the setting as ideal "for a city destined to grow great."

Whether or not Romulus really existed and became a Roman king, we do know that the first rulers of Rome came from both the Etruscans and the Latins. The first three, so inscriptions and records tell us, were Numa Pompilius (a Sabine), Tullus Hostilius (a Latin), and Ancus Martius (a Sabine).

They were followed by three Etruscan kings: Lucius Tarquinius Priscus, Servius Tullius, and Lucius Tarquinius. The last one was nicknamed Superbus, which meant "The Proud." The people of Rome hated him and his arrogant rule, which lasted for about 25 years. They threw him out and established a completely different form of government for themselves.

▲ The "Capitoline Wolf." The she-wolf kept Romulus and Remus alive by suckling them. This bronze statue was made by an Etruscan artist in the sixth century B.C.E. The twins were added in the early 16th century C.E., but it is likely that there were others there originally.

◄ This Roman symbol was borrowed from the Etruscans. The ax and bundle of rods represented the power of consuls.

▼ Rome's allies and colonies. Allies supplied troops. Colonies were set up by Roman citizens.

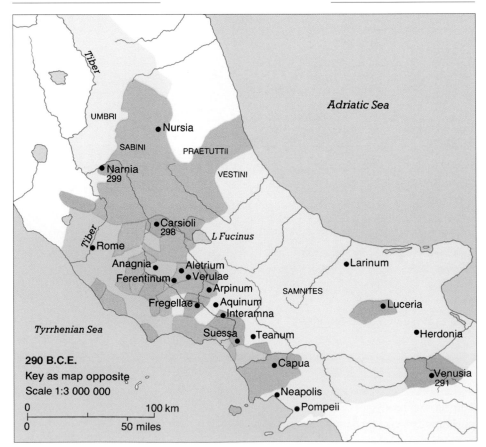

290 B.C.E.
Key as map opposite
Scale 1:3 000 000

0 _____ 100 km
0 _____ 50 miles

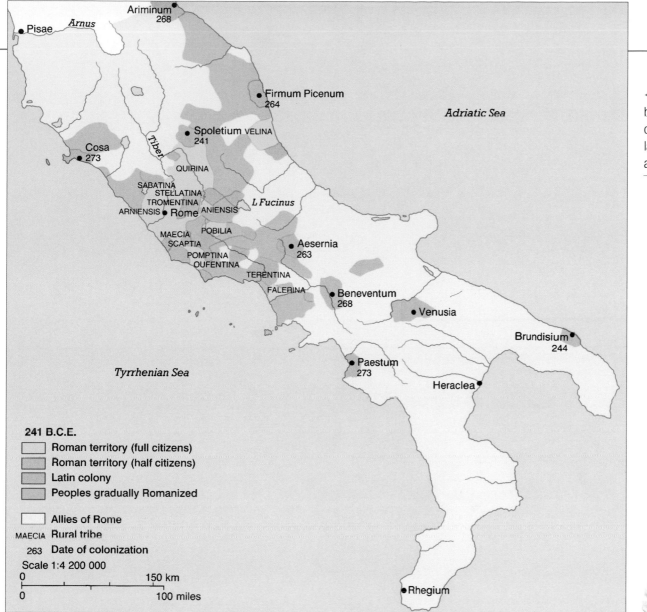

241 B.C.E.

☐ Roman territory (full citizens)
▨ Roman territory (half citizens)
▨ Latin colony
▨ Peoples gradually Romanized

☐ Allies of Rome
MAECIA Rural tribe
263 Date of colonization
Scale 1:4 200 000

Government by elections

The Romans called their new form of government *respublica* (our word "republic"). It literally meant "a matter for the people," and that was what the government was. Each year two officials, called consuls, were elected by the citizens.

Consuls had much the same power as kings. They were heads of government and they were in charge of the army. However, they were in office for only one year and they had to agree with each other about what to do.

Other officials were brought in to do the other jobs of government. Praetors were chief judges; censors kept the register of citizens who were entitled to vote; quaestors looked after the state's finances; and aediles were in charge of all public works. The senate, made up of ex-officials, formed a parliament that discussed matters of state and advised the officials.

Citizens and conquest

The Roman people were divided into "classes." The patricians were the noble families who could trace their origins back to early Rome. The plebeians were the ordinary working people. They were entitled to vote but they could not hold high office such as the consulship. Later, a new class emerged—the equites ("knights"), who were property-owning business men.

Although the state was a republic (there was no longer a king) and the system of government was democracy, not everyone could vote: slaves and women were excluded.

At first the new Roman state had friendly relations with its neighbors. Gradually, however, the Romans forced them to become part of their state, sometimes simply by conquering them. In this way a pattern of expansion began that would produce one of the world's greatest empires, which eventually included about 60 million people.

▲ A Samnite warrior from the sixth or fifth century B.C.E. He is fully protected with chest and leg armor. The Romans copied the idea of the long rectangular shield from these Samnites.

War with Carthage

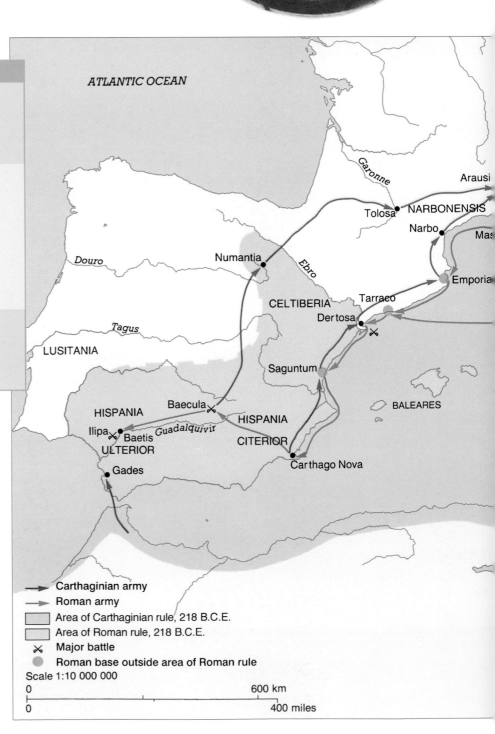

THE ROMAN REPUBLIC WENT FROM strength to strength. The armies of Rome conquered all of Italy. After several attempts, they also finally defeated King Pyrrhus of Epirus at Beneventum in 275 B.C.E. and became a major force to be reckoned with in the Mediterranean region. But they would discover that they were not the only "world power" there.

The Carthaginians' territory covered North Africa and part of Spain. Carthage then began to conquer Sicily, the large island close to the "toe" of Italy.

▶ "The elephants were of great use to the Carthaginians. The enemy were too terrified of their appearance to come anywhere near them."
Polybius, Roman historian.

Battles between Rome and Carthage

First war
264 B.C.E. Carthage occupies Messana. Romans defeat the Carthaginians and occupy the town.
260 B.C.E. Rome builds its fleet. Full-scale war.
241 B.C.E. Carthage surrenders.

Second war
221 B.C.E. Hannibal made Carthaginian commander-in-chief.
219 B.C.E. Saguntum captured. Rome declares war.
218 B.C.E. Hannibal marches across the Alps. Romans defeated at Ticino and Trebia Rivers.
217 B.C.E. Two Roman legions lost at Lake Trasimeno.
216 B.C.E. Rome's worst defeat, at Cannae.
204 B.C.E. Romans invade North Africa.
202 B.C.E. Carthage defeated at Zama.
183 B.C.E. Hannibal commits suicide.

Third war
149 B.C.E. War breaks out again.
146 B.C.E. City of Carthage completely destroyed. North Africa becomes a Roman province.

The first war

When the Carthaginians occupied the town of Messana (modern Messina) the Romans sent two legions of soldiers there and defeated them. Full-scale war then broke out. For 20 years the two mighty nations fought each other.

A few years later the Romans moved into Corsica and Sardinia. The war ended in 241 B.C.E. with a battle off the west coast of Sicily. Rome occupied Sicily and made it its first province.

Hannibal—enemy of Rome

Hamilcar had been the Carthaginian commander at the end of the first war against Rome. In 237 B.C.E. he led an army into Spain to conquer new territory and defend Carthaginian settlements already there. Spain provided the Carthaginians with rich supplies

Carthaginian army
Roman army
Area of Carthaginian rule, 218 B.C.E.
Area of Roman rule, 218 B.C.E.
✗ **Major battle**
● **Roman base outside area of Roman rule**
Scale 1:10 000 000
0 — 600 km
0 — 400 miles

◄ The Carthaginians were a seafaring trading nation with a large navy. The Romans had to build a fleet especially to fight them. First they built 120 ships such as these, later another 200. Off the Aegates Islands west of Sicily the Romans sank 50 Carthaginian warships laden with supplies for the troops and captured 70 more. The rest of the fleet escaped, but Carthage was beaten.

▼ Campaign routes of the two "world powers." Both the Romans and the Carthaginians needed an efficient navy. At first the Carthaginians had the naval advantage. Both sides also needed wealth to pay for the expensive wars and for their allies.

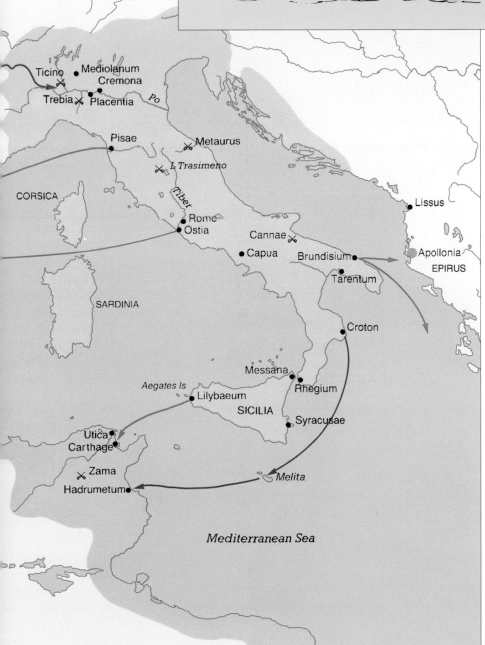

of farm produce and metals with which they fed and equipped their armies.

> "*Hamilcar was about to cross to Spain with his army and was making sacrifices. Hannibal, then about nine years old, was childishly teasing his father to take him too. His father, still angry at the loss of Sicily and Sardinia, led him to the altar and made him swear to be the enemy of Rome as soon as he was able.*"— the historian Livy.

Hamilcar's son, Hannibal, took over control of Carthaginian forces in Spain in 221 B.C.E. He was only 25 years old. After two years he conquered the town of Saguntum, Rome's ally. The Romans sent two armies against the Carthaginians: one to Carthage, and the other to Massilia (now Marseille).

Crossing the Alps

Hannibal astonished the Romans by marching to Italy across the Alps. No Roman believed he would take this route. His huge army of 40,000 men also had 37 war elephants with them.

It was a hard march, and Hannibal reached Italy with only 26,000 men and 12 elephants remaining. However, he brought in more troops and with an army of about 50,000 began to defeat the Romans in their own country.

Rome saved

A new Roman general, Publius Cornelius Scipio, was appointed to cope with this crisis. He went to attack Carthage and forced Hannibal to fight him there. Hannibal's army was defeated at Zama in 202 B.C.E.

The Legions

THE ROMANS NEEDED A LARGE ARMY to conquer all the areas they wanted to rule and to defeat enemies such as the Carthaginian Hannibal. At first the Roman soldiers were part-time. Men were called up for duty whenever an army was needed.

Not every man was called to serve, however. Only Roman citizens between the ages of 17 and 46 who owned some property were allowed to be soldiers. Later in the history of Rome men volunteered to become full-time soldiers and sailors and served for at least 20 years.

Army organization

Over the years the way in which the army fought gradually changed. New tactics were invented or copied from other armies. The soldiers were organized into large units called legions. Soldiers were known as legionaries.

For marching, training, and fighting, the soldiers operated in smaller groups of about 100 men, commanded by a centurion. (The English word "century," meaning 100, comes from the Latin word.)

▲ Roman soldiers battling with tribesmen of Dacia in the second century C.E. Notice how well armed and protected the Romans are, with their helmets and armor.

A legionary's load

A legionary carried about 66 lb (30 kg) of kit on the march. It included tools for building camp, bags to hold a saw, chain, rope, and provisions, pots and pans for cooking, and a leather shield cover.

Soldiers were trained not only to fight but also to build the forts and roads needed to hold conquered territory.

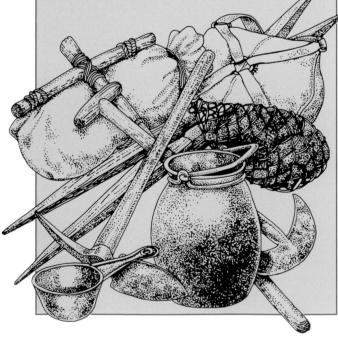

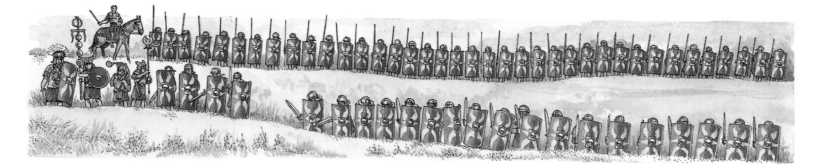

Weapons and uniform

Roman soldiers fought with long spears and swords. Over the years their uniform and armor changed. In the early years of Rome a legionary often wore a helmet with long plumes of feathers, carried an oval-shaped shield, and was protected by a short suit of chain mail.

Later the shape of the shield changed, and the full-time soldier in the second century C.E. had plates of metal joined together into armor to protect his upper body. A legionary's helmet now had flaps to protect his cheeks and neck.

▲ When preparing for battle, soldiers equipped with swords and spears would form protective ranks in front of cavalry and archers.

◀ This soldier is equipped for a march. In addition to the items shown (far left) he carried rations for three days.

▲ On a march through enemy territory, the army would build a camp each night, fortified by banks and wooden walls.

▲ In the foreground stands a centurion, the leader of a small army group. Beside him is a *signifer,* who carried the group's standard or emblem, the *signum.*

Early Years of Crisis

IN THE SECOND CENTURY B.C.E. THERE WAS a serious threat to Rome on its northern and eastern borders. The northern tribes—Cimbri, Teutones, and Ambrones—made Spain, southern Gaul, and even Italy unsafe. In 105 B.C.E. a whole Roman army was slaughtered at Arausio by these northern warriors.

In the east Mithridates VI, king of Pontus, occupied Asia and the Greek islands. He was welcomed in the Roman territory of Asia in 88 B.C.E., where the people had been treated very badly by their Roman masters. Mithridates was defeated by Rome in 63 B.C.E.

Another threat to Rome came from large bands of pirates who were based in the area of the eastern Mediterranean. The Roman commander Pompey finally defeated them in 67 B.C.E.

Unrest and hostility in the empire

In the west and north
133 B.C.E. After 70 years of war Rome finally defeats the local people at Numantia in Spain.
113 B.C.E. Cimbri defeat Romans at Noreia.
105 B.C.E. Roman army slaughtered at Arausio.
102 B.C.E. Teutones defeated at Aquae Sextiae.
101 B.C.E. Cimbri defeated at Vercellae.

In the east and Africa
146 B.C.E. Corinth, capital city of Achaea in Greece, destroyed by the Romans.
133 B.C.E. Roman province of Asia formed.
112 B.C.E. War with Numidian king Jugurtha. Roman victory in 105 B.C.E.
88 B.C.E. King Mithridates occupies Asia, but it is regained by the Roman general Sulla in 85 B.C.E.
86 B.C.E. Sulla captures Athens for Rome.

Around Italy
136–132 and 104–101 B.C.E. Slave uprisings in Sicily against the Romans.
126–122 and 115–111 B.C.E. Revolts in Sardinia.
91–89 B.C.E. War against rebellious allies in Italy.

▼ From 146 to 70 B.C.E. Rome faced difficulties throughout its empire. The period of crisis ended only when ambitious men such as Marius, Sulla, and Pompey became powerful.

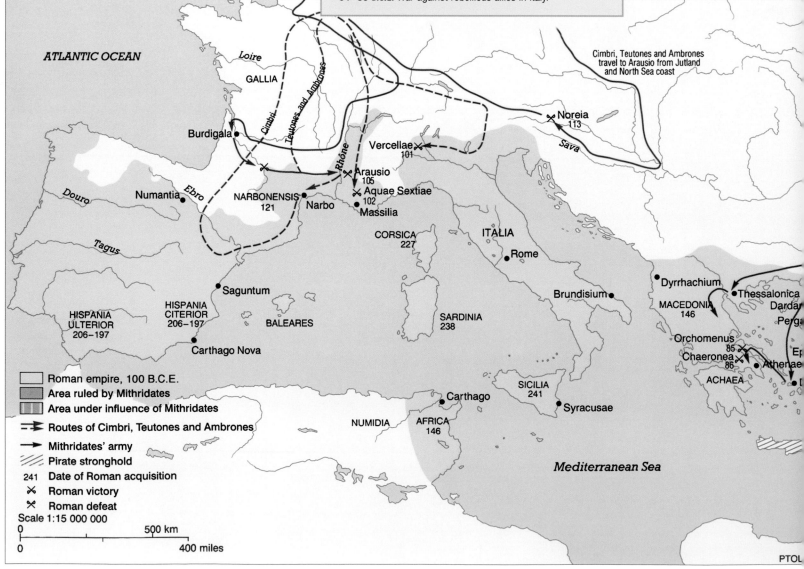

Roman empire, 100 B.C.E.
Area ruled by Mithridates
Area under influence of Mithridates
Routes of Cimbri, Teutones and Ambrones
Mithridates' army
Pirate stronghold
241 Date of Roman acquisition
⤬ Roman victory
⤫ Roman defeat
Scale 1:15 000 000
0 — 500 km
0 — 400 miles

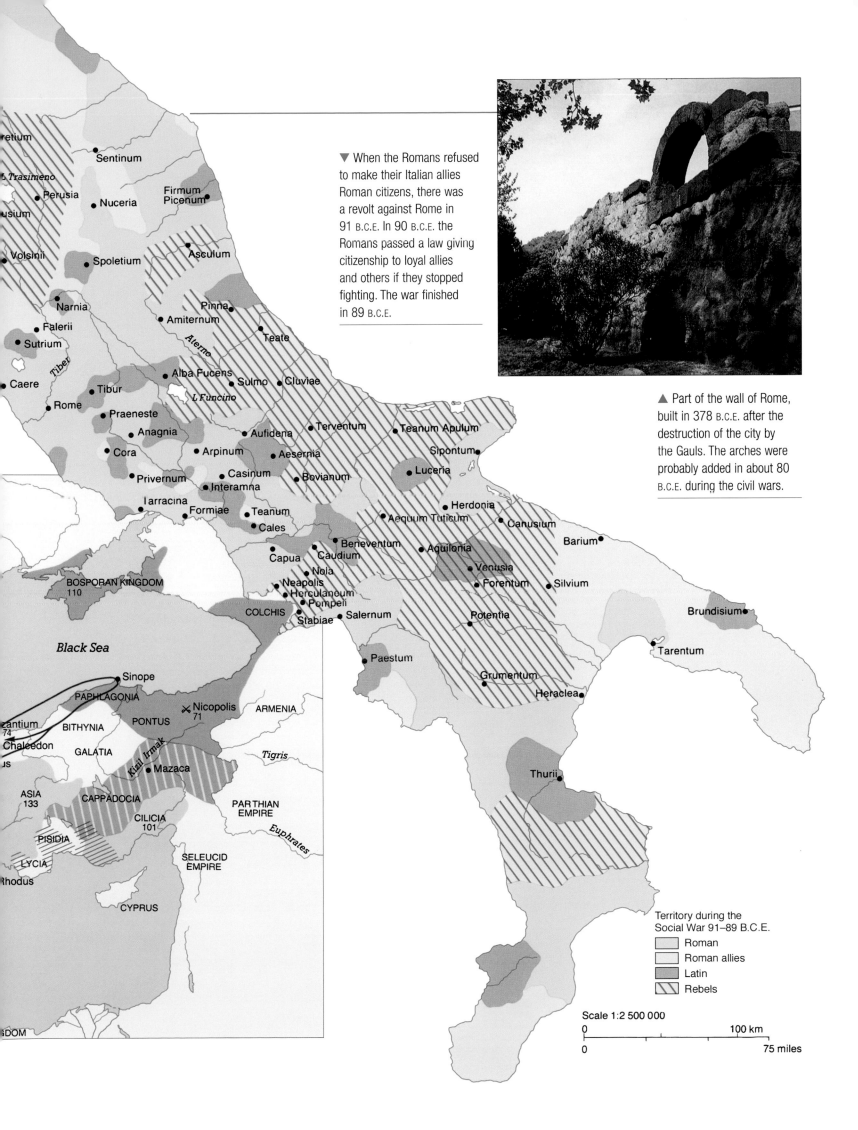

When the Romans refused to make their Italian allies Roman citizens, there was a revolt against Rome in 91 B.C.E. In 90 B.C.E. the Romans passed a law giving citizenship to loyal allies and others if they stopped fighting. The war finished in 89 B.C.E.

Part of the wall of Rome, built in 378 B.C.E. after the destruction of the city by the Gauls. The arches were probably added in about 80 B.C.E. during the civil wars.

retium
Sentinum
L. Trasimeno
Perusia
Nuceria
Firmum Picenum
usium
Volsinii
Spoletium
Asculum
Narnia
Pinna
Falerii
Amiternum
Sutrium
Aterno
Teate
Caere
Tiber
Alba Fucens
Sulmo
Cluviae
Tibur
L. Fucino
Rome
Praeneste
Anagnia
Terventum
Teanum Apulum
Cora
Aufidena
Sipontum
Arpinum
Aesernia
Privernum
Casinum
Bovianum
Luceria
Interamna
Tarracina
Formiae
Teanum
Herdonia
Cales
Aequum Tuticum
Canusium
Beneventum
Barium
Capua
Caudium
Aquilonia
Nola
Venusia
Neapolis
Forentum
Silvium
Herculaneum
Pompeii
Brundisium
COLCHIS
Salernum
Rotentia
Stabiae
Tarentum
Black Sea
Paestum
Grumentum
Sinope
Heraclea
PAPHLAGONIA
Nicopolis 71
ARMENIA
zantium 74
PONTUS
BITHYNIA
Chalcedon
us
GALATIA
Tigris
Kizil Irmak
Mazaca
Thurii
ASIA 133
CAPPADOCIA
PARTHIAN EMPIRE
CILICIA 101
Euphrates
PISIDIA
LYCIA
SELEUCID EMPIRE
Rhodus
CYPRUS
BOSPORAN KINGDOM 110

Territory during the Social War 91–89 B.C.E.

	Roman
	Roman allies
	Latin
	Rebels

Scale 1:2 500 000

0 ———————— 100 km

0 ———————— 75 miles

Republican Rome

The seven hills of Rome

It is known that as early as 1000 B.C.E. there were separate small villages built on the seven hills that later made up the area of the capital city of the Roman state. The area that developed into the forum, Rome's trading and business center, was first built in around 600 B.C.E. Under Etruscan rule the villages became one community—the first town of Rome, which was founded in about 575 B.C.E.

The town grew, and the valleys which ran down to the Tiber River soon filled with buildings. The river led to the sea, where the port of Ostia was established. About 378 B.C.E. a wall was built to enclose and protect Rome. This Servian Wall was originally thought to have been built by an early Roman king, Servius Tullius. The city was never formally planned out, unlike later Roman towns, especially in the provinces.

▼ Republican Rome. The dotted line of the Aurelian Wall shows the city's extent by the late third century C.E. Details of the city's first stone theater (inset right), built by Pompey in 55 B.C.E., survive on a marble plan of the city.

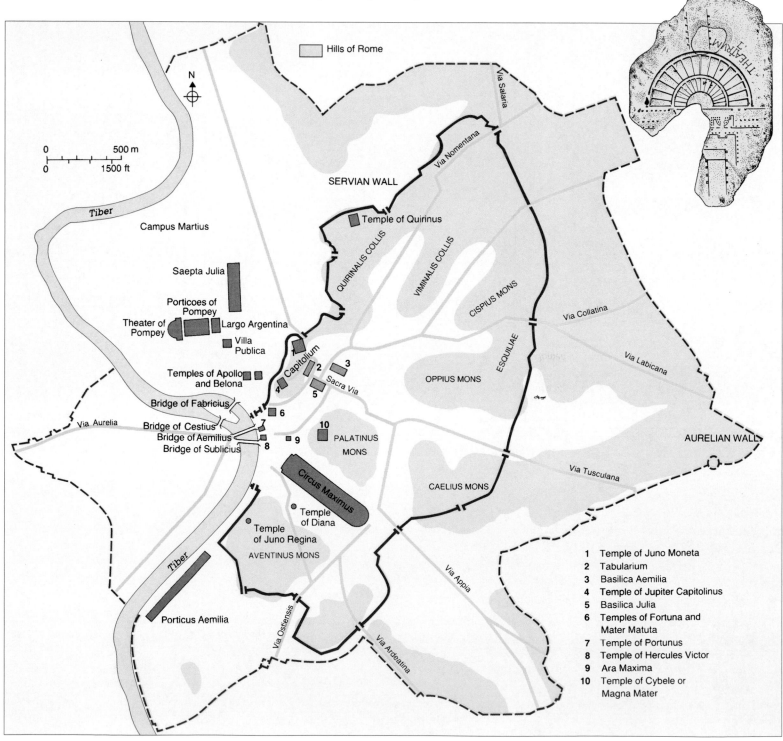

Hills of Rome

SERVIAN WALL

Tiber

Campus Martius

Saepta Julia

Porticoes of Pompey

Theater of Pompey

Largo Argentina

Villa Publica

Temples of Apollo and Belona

Capitolium

Sacra Via

Temple of Quirinus

QUIRINALIS COLLIS

VIMINALIS COLLIS

CISPIUS MONS

Via Salaria

Via Nomentana

Via Collatina

Via Labicana

ESQUILIAE

OPPIUS MONS

Bridge of Fabricius

Via Aurelia

Bridge of Cestius

Bridge of Aemilius

Bridge of Sublicius

PALATINUS MONS

AURELIAN WALL

Via Tusculana

Circus Maximus

CAELIUS MONS

Temple of Diana

Temple of Juno Regina

AVENTINUS MONS

Tiber

Via Appia

Via Ostensis

Via Ardeatina

Porticus Aemilia

1 Temple of Juno Moneta
2 Tabularium
3 Basilica Aemilia
4 Temple of Jupiter Capitolinus
5 Basilica Julia
6 Temples of Fortuna and Mater Matuta
7 Temple of Portunus
8 Temple of Hercules Victor
9 Ara Maxima
10 Temple of Cybele or Magna Mater

Rome expands

Rome had around 100,000 inhabitants in the third century B.C.E. This number rose rapidly to nearly 1 million in Julius Caesar's time. Although the poor still lived in ramshackle accommodation in the valleys, the rich had moved to the cooler, healthier hills. The Roman lawyer and philosopher Cicero wrote, "Two of my apartment buildings have fallen down . . . even the mice have moved out!"

The huge population needed fresh water in vast quantities. Many aqueducts were built to bring water from the hills to the heart of Rome. A network of roads was developed, providing main highways through the city and across Italy.

Public buildings

By the end of the fourth century B.C.E., Rome had become an important and very wealthy town. Splendid buildings surrounded the first forum, and other public squares were built. The city center had a number of fine temples.

By the first century B.C.E., 100,000 people could watch chariot-racing in the Circus Maximus. Near the river and the marketplaces great warehouses and trading centers, such as the Porticus Aemilia, were constructed.

Not many of the monuments and buildings built during the republic survive today. They were replaced by those erected under the emperors.

▲ Great stone aqueducts were built to bring water into Rome from the hills. The water was carried in a channel on the top. Rome's first aqueduct was built by the politician Appius Claudius in 312 B.C.E. It was called the Aqua Appia. The same man also built the Via Appia, a road from Rome to Capua.

The Rise of Julius Caesar

JULIUS CAESAR CLAIMED THAT HE WAS descended from the gods. He said that Aeneas, the Trojan hero and son of the goddess Venus, was his ancestor. Surviving records suggest that he was born between 102 and 100 B.C.E. into an important family of the patrician class. He was related by marriage to Marius, a politician and an enemy of the dictator Sulla during the civil war of 83 B.C.E. This connection helped his career but it also brought him into conflict with Sulla.

A career in the state's service

Like so many other Roman aristocrats, Julius Caesar began his career in the army, serving in the eastern empire. On his return to Rome he began his political career by taking various public offices, such as head of financial affairs in Spain.

Later he was in charge of all public building in Rome, chief priest, and a governor in Spain. Finally he was elected as consul in 60 B.C.E. For one year he shared with a fellow consul complete control of the government and army.

Conquest of Gaul

After his consulship Caesar could choose which province he wanted to govern. He went in 58 B.C.E. to govern the provinces in northern Italy and Gaul. He decided to campaign against the Celtic people and not only make Roman territory safer but increase it. Cicero, a famous orator and philosopher, said of him in a speech to the senate:

"Before, members of the senate, we only had a route through Gaul. All the other territories were occupied by peoples who either were hostile to us or could not be trusted. Caesar has fought very successfully against the fiercest of peoples in great battles and made them part of the Roman state."

Civil war and after

Because of these successful military campaigns, Julius Caesar became popular but aroused jealousy. When in 49 B.C.E. his rival Pompey persuaded the senate to order him to disband his army, civil war broke out. It ended four years later when Caesar defeated Pompey's sons in Spain. Caesar was now the most powerful person in Rome and declared himself "dictator for life."

Rome was no longer a republic with people able to vote for their leaders, and to some it was obvious that Caesar wanted an end to democracy. He also wanted for himself the supreme title of *rex*—king. Marcus Brutus, Gaius Cassius, and others plotted to kill Caesar, and on March 15, 44 B.C.E., they stabbed him to death outside the senate house.

▲ A portrait of Julius Caesar in middle age, carved in marble. The Roman writer Suetonius said that Caesar was *"a bit of a dandy. He always had his hair carefully trimmed and used to comb his few hairs forward to cover his baldness."*

▼ Carthage in North Africa was completely destroyed by Rome in 146 B.C.E., ending the war with the Carthaginian Empire. Caesar later made it a colony for retired soldiers.

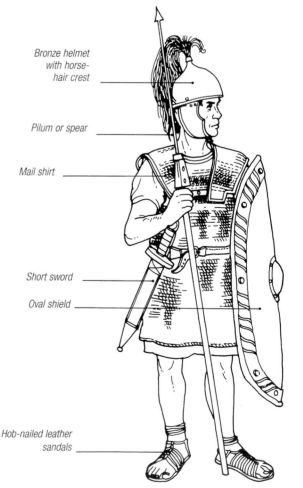

Bronze helmet with horse-hair crest

Pilum or spear

Mail shirt

Short sword

Oval shield

Hob-nailed leather sandals

◄ The most important public buildings in Rome were sited in the Forum Romanum. On the right are the ruins of the Basilica Julia—a great meeting hall built by Caesar.

► Coins often pictured great events in Roman history. Above is the coin minted in 48 B.C.E. to celebrate Caesar's victories in Gaul. The one below commemorates his murder, with the date, the "Ides of March."

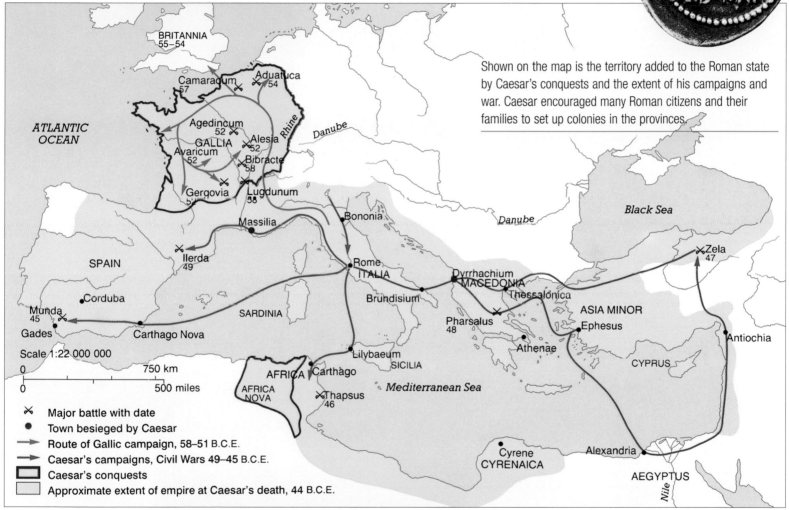

Shown on the map is the territory added to the Roman state by Caesar's conquests and the extent of his campaigns and war. Caesar encouraged many Roman citizens and their families to set up colonies in the provinces.

BRITANNIA 55–54

Camaracum 57

Aduatuca 54

Agedincum 52

Alesia 52

GALLIA

Avaricum 52

Bibracte 58

Gergovia 52

Lugdunum 58

ATLANTIC OCEAN

Rhine

Danube

Massilia

Bononia

Danube

Black Sea

SPAIN

Ilerda 49

Rome ITALIA

Dyrrhachium MACEDONIA

Thessalonica

ASIA MINOR

Zela 47

Corduba

Brundisium

Pharsalus 48

Ephesus

Antiochia

Munda 45

SARDINIA

Athenae

CYPRUS

Gades

Carthago Nova

Lilybaeum

SICILIA

Mediterranean Sea

Scale 1:22 000 000

0   750 km

0   500 miles

AFRICA

Carthago

AFRICA NOVA

Thapsus 46

Cyrene CYRENAICA

Alexandria

AEGYPTUS

Nile

✕ Major battle with date
● Town besieged by Caesar
→ Route of Gallic campaign, 58–51 B.C.E.
→ Caesar's campaigns, Civil Wars 49–45 B.C.E.
▭ Caesar's conquests
▭ Approximate extent of empire at Caesar's death, 44 B.C.E.

◄ A full-time professional soldier. Julius Caesar could not have conquered so much new territory for the Roman state without such men.

► The forum of Caesar. The main building was a temple of Venus. A statue of the dictator on horseback stood in the center of the square.

Caesar wins the civil war of 49–45 B.C.E.

49 B.C.E. Caesar marches on Rome. In Spain he destroys Pompey's army at Ilerda. Pompey flees to Greece.

48 B.C.E. At Dyrrhachium, Pompey breaks through Caesar's defenses, but Caesar defeats him at the great battle of Pharsalus. Pompey is pursued to Egypt and is murdered before Caesar arrives.

47 B.C.E. Caesar establishes Cleopatra as queen in Egypt. He marches through Syria and Asia Minor to defeat Pompey's ally, Pharnaces of Pontus, at Zela.

46 B.C.E. Caesar adds Africa Nova to the empire after defeating Pompey's two sons at Thapsus.

45 B.C.E. He defeats the Pompeian army at Munda.

Roman Men and Women

A LARGE AMOUNT OF EVIDENCE SURVIVES to show us what Roman men and women looked like. The Romans liked sculpture, especially in stone. Stone statues and busts of emperors, gods and goddesses, and famous people were erected in the streets, public buildings, and temples. Wealthy Romans had statues or busts of their ancestors in their homes.

We also find carved portraits on Roman tombstones and burial vaults. This tells us not only what people looked like but sometimes what they did. They might be pictured at work—a shoemaker, for example—or dressed in the clothes for their job—a soldier perhaps.

Tombstones often give us other information about Roman people or their life. On a tombstone you might find a portrait of a woman with her family seated around a table, also her name and where she came from. Tombstones of tradespeople or soldiers usually give us details about what their work was.

Portraits of emperors usually appear on Roman coins as well as on statues. Because rulers tend to want a bit of flattery in their official portraits, these may not always be true likenesses. The writer Suetonius said that the Emperor Claudius had "an uncontrollable laugh when angry, slobbered at the mouth and had a runny nose," but this does not show in any of his statues.

▲ This bust shows a male hairstyle and close-cropped beard typical of the period.

▶ This man has the distinctive Roman hooked nose, which Romans found attractive.

◀ The tombstone of a young man from Palmyra in Syria who died in the second century C.E. He wears a toga. The inscription is in his own language, Syriac.

▶ The work of the blacksmith, pictured on a burial monument. On the left an assistant or apprentice heats up the forge with bellows. He is protected from the heat by a large shield. The blacksmith (center) sits at the anvil hammering an object into shape. On the right are his tools—tongs and hammer—and below them a spearhead and a door lock, two of his products.

► This lady from Pompeii wears gold earrings and what looks like a gold hairnet. She holds a "book" of wooden tablets, each covered with a thin layer of wax. Writing was done by marking the wax with the pointed stylus.

◄ A very elaborate hairstyle worn by a lady (probably in the emperor's court) of the first century C.E.

► This toga-clad greengrocer set up his stall in the port of Ostia, where this sculpture was found on a burial monument. There is a basket for the goods under the trestle table, and on top the vegetables look like garlic, leeks, and globe artichokes.

Hairstyles

Roman men and women of all classes took a great deal of care over their hair and appearance. Until the second century C.E. most men were clean shaven, but after that period beards became popular. Men's hair was sometimes cropped short, but it was usually combed slightly forward, as can be seen in the examples on these pages.

Women's hairstyles could be fairly simple but also included very elaborate curls, which must have occupied expert maids for a long time. Some women wore wigs or dyed their hair using extracts from plants, much as we do today. Women also used make-up consisting of chalk for a white skin and red ocher for lips and cheeks.

Clothes

In some parts of the Roman world men wore tight trousers but in most places they wore a tunic like the blacksmith's shown below. Roman citizens (only men could be citizens) could wear the toga—a large semicircular piece of cloth wrapped loosely around the upper body. This was a symbol of manhood as well as citizenship. Women wore undertunics with a dress called a *stola* on top. In the open air they might wear a *palla*, a loose-fitting garment.

Both men and women wore jewelry such as brooches, necklaces, and rings.

Pompeii—Struck by Disaster

"Everything is drowned in the flames and buried in the ashes of sadness."

SO WROTE THE ROMAN POET MARTIAL about the destruction of the towns in the Bay of Naples by the volcano Vesuvius in 79 C.E. Pompeii and Herculaneum suffered the worst. They suffered so much damage that they were never lived in again in the Roman period.

We know about the destruction because an eyewitness recorded the events. The writer Pliny was staying with his uncle, a commander of the Roman fleet stationed near by, and saw an extraordinary cloud in the sky. He noted:

"On August 24 at about 1 p.m., my mother pointed out to Uncle an odd-shaped cloud. We could not make out which mountain it came from but later found out that it was from Vesuvius. The cloud was rising in a shape like a pine tree because it shot up to a great height in the form of a tall trunk, then spread out at the top into branches."

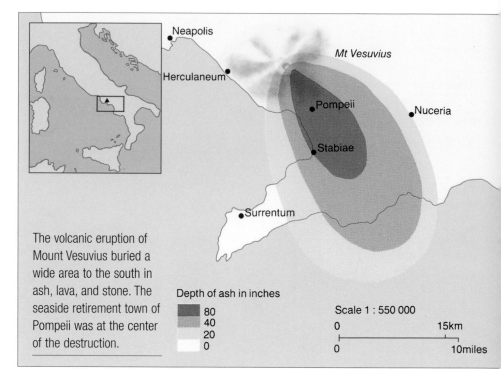

The volcanic eruption of Mount Vesuvius buried a wide area to the south in ash, lava, and stone. The seaside retirement town of Pompeii was at the center of the destruction.

Depth of ash in inches

▓	80
▓	40
░	20
	0

Scale 1 : 550 000

0   15km

0   10miles

▲ ▼ The excavator Fiorelli poured liquid plaster into the holes left by bodies enclosed in ash from Vesuvius. These people were probably overcome by fumes and must have suffocated to death. Casts sometimes show details of clothing and footwear.

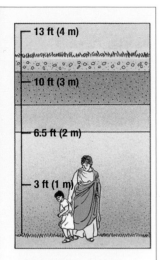

▲ Vesuvius deposited ash and stone on top of Pompeii. A mud flow 66 ft (20m) deep covered the town of Herculaneum.

When the top of Vesuvius blew up, it rained down ash, stone, and lava over a wide area. Some places such as Naples had just a thin coating of ash, but Pompeii was covered to a depth of nearly 13 feet (4 m). About 2,000 people (from a population of 20,000) lost their lives—either crushed, trapped in buildings, or suffocated by the sulfur fumes. At Herculaneum the volcanic eruption caused a mud flow that completely covered all the buildings.

It took about three days for the sky to clear and by then it was no longer possible to live in the towns. The emperor Titus gave money for the relief of the refugees, but the towns were never rebuilt.

Rediscovery of a Roman town

Pompeii and Herculaneum were forgotten during the Roman period. They were not rediscovered until the 16th century. By the 18th century people had begun to excavate them. The excavations turned into hunting parties for beautiful objects, such as statues and mosaics.

A great deal of Pompeii and some of Herculaneum was dug up. These first excavations revealed parts of houses, shops, streets, and public buildings that had been buried. The work was very careless, though, and some of the remains were damaged. In 1860 the new director of excavations, Giuseppe Fiorelli, began to uncover large areas instead of digging holes everywhere. He carried out his work with care and often succeeded in preserving whole buildings.

Town plan

Pompeii probably gives us the most detailed picture we have of a prosperous Roman town in the first century C.E. It was originally an Etruscan town but was redeveloped several times.

Much of the town was divided into regular blocks called *insulae* ("islands"). The town had a large forum (or marketplace)—that also contained the town's offices, market halls, and temples—as well as two theaters, an amphitheater, and several bath houses enclosed by a stone wall.

◀ An aerial view of the town center of Pompeii. The main roadway is paved, with wide walkways on either side. Most houses had a blank wall facing the street, to protect privacy, with just a simple doorway. Some of the buildings have been reconstructed.

▼ Stepping stones helped people cross the dirty, wet streets. There were a number of shops opening straight onto the street.

The Empire of Augustus

THE ROMANS STILL TALKED ABOUT THE republic and voted for their officials, but in reality the state had been in the hands of a few powerful men for many years. Politicians like Sulla, Pompey, and Julius Caesar seized power, backed by their own troops.

Caesar had increased the size of the Roman Empire enormously. His murder caused another civil war. His adopted son and heir Octavian came back from Greece, where he was studying, to avenge his father's death.

The empire divided

After several battles across the empire the winners, Octavian and Marcus Antonius (usually called Mark

▼ Statue of the emperor Augustus in a general's uniform, aged about 45. The breastplate shows a defeated barbarian and a Roman officer.

Antony now), divided the Roman world between them. Antony ruled the east from his base in Alexandria, Egypt, where he could be with his love Queen Cleopatra. Octavian ruled from Rome.

Neither Octavian nor the senate of Rome would allow the Roman state to remain split. War was declared against Cleopatra and Antony in 31 B.C.E. Octavian won the war and declared peace for the Romans in 29 B.C.E.

Mighty Augustus

Octavian was now all-powerful in the Roman state and in 27 B.C.E. was given the title Augustus ("a person to be respected") by the senate, along with the legal power to rule Rome's religious, civil and military affairs, with the senate as an advisory body. In the same year, writes the geographer Strabo:

> "Augustus divided the whole of his empire into two parts, giving one portion to the Roman people and keeping the other portion to govern himself."

Augustus used the Roman legions to secure the empire's frontiers in Spain and Germany. Some provinces now had governors appointed by the senate (senatorial provinces). The others (imperial provinces) had governors appointed by Augustus.

Augustus formed an elite force just to protect him, called the praetorian guard. There may have been as many as 9,000 of these soldiers based in Rome and loyal only to the emperor.

Governing the provinces

Augustus had chosen his provinces carefully. They were the ones where most of the armies were stationed. He also chose carefully the people to govern those provinces. He wanted governors who would be loyal to him.

Augustus kept Egypt as his own personal property and had a law passed forbidding any senator from entering the country without his permission.

The governor's staff

The governor's title in Latin was *Legatus* ("appointed person") *Augusti* ("by Augustus the Emperor") *pro Praetore* ("in his place as governor").

The governor was commander-in-chief and had 30 to 40 officials under him. An official called a procurator looked after the province's finances, and there were military staff, secretaries, messengers, couriers, personal assistants, lawyers, and clerks.

▶ Part of the Altar of the Peace of Augustus, put up by the senate in Augustus' honor in 13 B.C.E. The carving shows members of the imperial family taking part in annual sacrifices at the altar.

▼ The Roman Empire in 27 B.C.E. In the provinces people's way of life became "romanized." In 22 B.C.E. Augustus claimed that Narbonensis in Gaul was "more a part of Italy than a province." Legions of the Roman army were stationed throughout the empire (only a few remained in Italy), and this helped the spread of Roman customs.

ATLANT
OCEA

TARRACON
Douro
LUSITANIA
Tagus

BAETICA

Senatorial province
Imperial province
Scale 1:20 000 000
0
0
600 km
400 miles

Augustus, the first emperor

March 15, 44 B.C.E. Julius Caesar murdered. Civil war breaks out.

31 B.C.E. Mark Antony and Cleopatra defeated by Octavian at the battle of Actium in Achaen.

January 11, 29 B.C.E. Octavian declares peace throughout the Roman world.

28 B.C.E. Octavian appointed *Princeps Senatus* ("leader of the senate"). He is now in control of the state's armies and its finances.

27 B.C.E. Octavian given the title Augustus. The eighth month, *sextilis*, is now renamed *augustus*.

23 B.C.E. Augustus takes complete control of all the provinces. After this he takes on more and more of the power of elected officials. The senate grants him extended powers.

15–13 B.C.E. Augustus lives in Gaul.

2 B.C.E. Augustus is granted the title *Pater Patriae* ("father of the country").

August 19, 14 C.E. Augustus dies at Nola.

September 17, 14 C.E. The senate decrees that the emperor Augustus is one of the gods of Rome.

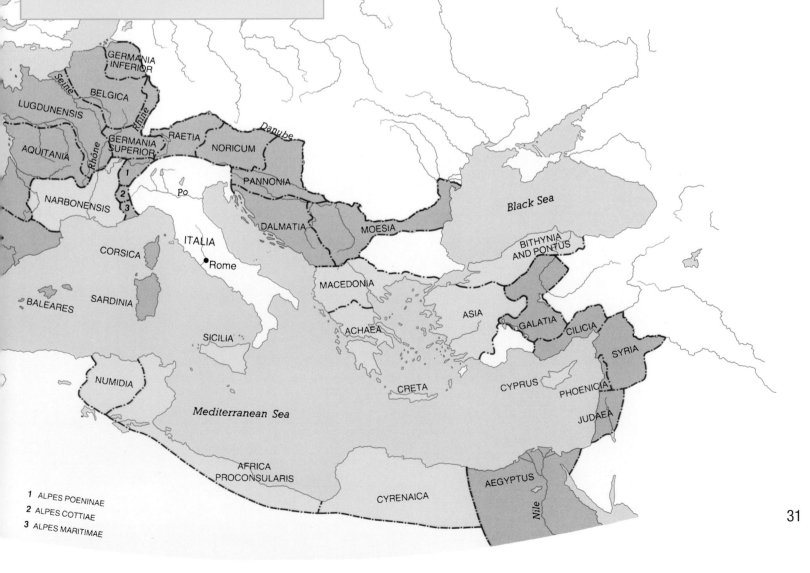

1 ALPES POENINAE
2 ALPES COTTIAE
3 ALPES MARITIMAE

Trajan's Army

THE EMPEROR TRAJAN BUILT A GREAT monument to the Roman army. He erected a huge column, covered with carvings, in the center of Rome. It was a record of his conquest of Dacia, north of the Danube River.

The column's fine carvings show us what Roman soldiers and their enemies looked like, how they fought, how they built their camps and the religious traditions that were key to their daily lives. Trajan's wars made Dacia a new Roman province in 106 C.E.

Defending the frontiers

Once a new province was made part of the Roman Empire it had to be defended. Large armies were left behind to patrol the conquered country. They had to build permanent forts to live in, with sturdy defensive walls. Hadrian's Wall was built along Britain's northern frontier, and similar walls were constructed along the Rhine and Danube Rivers.

A fort was laid out in a very regular way with easy access to its walls and gates. The legionaries lived in barrack blocks built for units of about 80 to 100 men, with a centurion in charge. Other buildings inside the fort included the headquarters, hospital, various workshops, and stores.

The soldier's life

In the provinces a soldier had plenty of other work to do apart from fighting. In Egypt, for example, besides training and building roads or forts, detachments from the legions were sent out on guard duty at frontiers (to ensure that customs dues were paid), at mines and quarries, at road junctions, and at grain supply depots. These examples are taken from the records of a legion in about 80 C.E.:

"Marcus Papirius Rufus—assigned to the granary in the Neapolis district of Alexandria as a secretary; Titus Saturnius—to harbor dredging; Titus Valens— to papyrus manufacture; Titus Celer—to the river patrol boat."

The emperor Trajan did not always approve of soldiers doing "civilian" jobs. He made this very clear when he wrote to the governor of Bithynia in 111 C.E.:

"There is no need to withdraw any soldiers to guard the prisons. It is much better to observe our ancient custom of employing public slaves for this purpose— as few soldiers as possible should be taken off their normal duties."

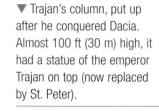

▼ Trajan's column, put up after he conquered Dacia. Almost 100 ft (30 m) high, it had a statue of the emperor Trajan on top (now replaced by St. Peter).

▲ Soldiers shown building a fortified camp—a detail from Trajan's column. A soldier on the left keeps watch. The men's swords, helmets, and shields are near by (far right). Some (right) dig out the defensive ditch and build a rampart, carrying the earth in baskets. Others strengthen the bank with wooden beams. The wall is made from squares of turf.

Trajan stands inside the wall at the top, waiting for a Dacian prisoner (bottom left) to be brought up. The clothes of the two soldiers who are leading him by the hair show that they are auxiliary soldiers, recruited locally. To the left, more legionaries build a bridge over a stream, beyond which a sentry guards another camp.

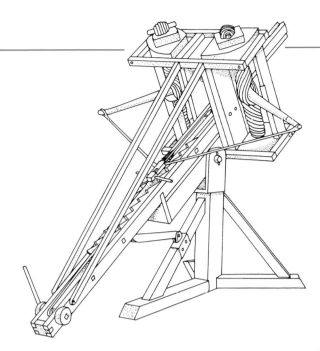

◀ This artillery machine was called a *ballista*. Like a crossbow on a stand, it fired short, iron-tipped bolts with great accuracy.

▶ As protection against missiles, Roman soldiers would link shields together and make a roof of them so strong that other soldiers could walk over it. This was called the *testudo*, or "tortoise," formation.

▶ This drawing, taken from a scene on Trajan's column, shows the siege of Sarmizegethusa, the native capital of Dacia. Both legionary soldiers and auxiliaries are storming the walls of a Dacian stronghold. As well as the *testudo*, *ballista*, and *onager* (stone-hurling machine), the Romans used siege towers and huge iron-headed battering rams mounted inside sheds on wheels.

Provinces and Frontiers

SEVERAL EMPERORS AFTER AUGUSTUS added to the territory controlled by Rome. The emperor Claudius himself took part in the invasion of Britain in 43 C.E. and he brought Thracia and Mauretania into the empire. Trajan served in many parts of the empire as a soldier and as provincial governor before becoming emperor. He was later responsible for adding new territories, such as Dacia.

Guarding the new frontiers

By the second century, when the empire was at its largest, between 50 and 60 million people probably lived within its frontiers. There were only 30 legions and auxiliary troops to control this vast area—nearly 450,000 soldiers.

Some of these troops were stationed at frontiers, on Hadrian's Wall in Britain, for example. The emperor Hadrian, builder of that wall, traveled widely. He was interested in the provinces and wanted to make sure his frontiers were safe.

Roads and communications

The Roman Empire depended on efficient communications—especially roads that could be used all year around, even in wet winter weather. Troops had to be able to move quickly to trouble spots, and messages needed to be passed back to camps and to Rome.

Good roads and harbors were also necessary so that goods could be transported efficiently into and around the empire.

Imperial couriers

Augustus established an official courier service, the *cursus publicus*, to carry mail and people traveling on public business. It was expensive to maintain relays of horses and carriages on all the major routes through the empire. This was paid for, at least at first, by the cities and the towns that the roads passed through.

New provinces gained by Rome

Third century B.C.E.: 241 B.C.E. Sicilia. 238 B.C.E. Sardinia. 227 B.C.E. Corsica.

Second century B.C.E.: 146 B.C.E. Greece and Africa. 133–129 B.C.E. Asia. 121 B.C.E. Gallia Narbonensis. 101 B.C.E. Cilicia.

First century B.C.E.: 74 B.C.E. Cyrenaica. 68–67 B.C.E. Creta. 64–63 B.C.E. Syria, Bithynia, and Pontus.

58 B.C.E. Cyprus. 58–52 B.C.E. Gallia. 30 B.C.E. Aegyptus. 27 B.C.E. Spanish provinces. 25 B.C.E. Galatia. 15 B.C.E. Alpes Poeninae. 14 B.C.E. Alpes Maritimae. 16–9 B.C.E. Raetia, Noricum, Pannonia, and Dalmatia.

First and second centuries C.E. 6 C.E. Judaea. 17 C.E. Cappadocia. 40 C.E. Mauretania. 43 C.E. Britannia, Lycia, and Pamphylia. 46 C.E. Thracia. 58 C.E. Alpes Cottiae. 85–86 C.E. Moesia divided into two provinces. 90 C.E. Germania. 106 C.E. Arabia and Dacia.

▶ Provinces and frontiers of the empire to 106 C.E.

ATL OC

LUSITAN
Emerita Augusta ■
Corduba ■
BAET.

Tingi ■

MAURETAN. TINGITANA

Roman acquisition by
201 B.C.E.
100 B.C.E.
44 B.C.E.
14 C.E.
96 C.E.
106 C.E.

▲ Horse-drawn stage-coach with passengers on top and inside. Journeys were slow and dirty.

▶ Roman roads are often (but not always) straight. This one is in Carthage, North Africa.

On the road

Traveling officials were able to use the government rest-houses, *mansiones*. Others made do with

Travelers

roadside inns. People who were rich enough might travel in a litter, called a *lectica*, carried by four strong bearers. Journeys were slow by modern standards. Strong walkers could cover about 20 to 25 miles (32–40 km) in a day. Others traveled on horseback or by coach. The imperial post would shoot past, covering more than 40 miles (64 km) each day. The poet Horace commented about one journey: "We arrived quite worn out. It was to be expected. The journey was long, and the road conditions were awful because of heavy rain."

Supplies　　　　*Pedestrians and salesmen*　　　　*Wine tanker*　　　　*Despatch riders*

Men of Power: The Emperors

WHEN THE RULES, OR CONSTITUTION, of Roman government were first worked out, there was no word for "emperor." The Romans had always hated the word *rex* (king), because it offended their idea of democracy. They wanted republican rule, which meant rule through elected officials.

Last of the dictators

In times of crisis, however, the Romans would appoint a dictator. This was someone, usually a former consul, legally appointed to take full control of the government for a limited time. Julius Caesar was appointed dictator in 46 B.C.E.

When civil war ended in 31 B.C.E., it was clear that the vast Roman world could no longer be ruled by Roman democracy. Too many ambitious men, such as Caesar, had taken power for themselves with the backing of the army.

First of the emperors

The winner of the civil war was Augustus (born Octavian), grandson of Caesar's sister, and Caesar's adopted son. He became the first Roman emperor and established 30 years of peace.

From Augustus's time onward, formal titles were given to the emperor. The name Augustus, meaning "someone who is respected," was given to him by the senate in 27 B.C.E. He also took his adopted father's

▼ This coin pictures the joint emperors Diocletian and Maximian.

► Roman emperors, from Augustus to Justinian—and the end of the empire.

27 B.C.E.–14 C.E.	Augustus
14–37	Tiberius
37–41	Gaius Caligula
41–54	Claudius
54–68	Nero

68–69	Galba
69	Otho, Vitellius

69–79	Vespasian
79–81	Titus
81–96	Domitian
96–98	Nerva
97–117	Trajan (97–98 with Nerva)
117–38	Hadrian
138–61	Antoninus Pius
161–80	Marcus Aurelius (161–169 with Lucius Verus)
180–92	Commodus

193	Pertinax
193	Didius Julianus
193–211	Septimius Severus
211–17	Caracalla (211–212 with Geta)
217–18	Macrinus
218–22	Elagabalus
222–35	Alexander Severus

Time of disorder in the empire (235–284)

235–38	Maximinus
238	Gordian I and II (in Africa)
238	Balbinus and Pupienus (in Italy)
238–44	Gordian III
244–49	Philip
249–51	Decius
251–53	Trebonianus Gallus
253	Aemilianus
253–60	Valerian
253–68	Gallienus (253–260 with Valerian)

WEST		**EAST**	
259–74	Gallic empire of Postumus, Victorinus, Tetricus	260–72	Palmyrene empire of Odaenathus, Zenobia, Vaballath
268–70	Claudius		
270	Quintillus		
270–75	Aurelian		
275–76	Tacitus		
276–82	Probus		
282–83	Carus		
283–84	Carinus and Numerian		

284–305 Diocletian and Tetrarchy

WEST		EAST	
287–305	Maximian Augustus	284–305	Diocletian Augustus
293–305	Constantius Caesar	293–305	Galerius Caesar
305–06	Constantius Augustus	305–11	Galerius Augustus
305–06	Severus Caesar (306–07 Augustus)	305–09	Maximinus Caesar (309–13 Augustus)

306–12 Maxentius (Italy)

WEST		EAST	
306–07	Constantine Caesar (from 307 Augustus)	308–24	Licinius Augustus

312–24 Constantine joint emperor with Licinius

324–37 Constantine sole ruler

337–40 Constantine II **Constans** **337–61 Constantius II**

340–50 Constans
350–53 Magnentius (usurper)

351–54 Gallus Caesar

355–61 Jullan Caesar (360–63 Augustus)

361–63 Julian sole ruler
363–64 Jovian

364–75	Valentinian	364–78	Valens
375–83	Gratian	379–95	Theodosius

375–92 Valentinian II (Italy, Illyricum)

383–88	Maximus (usurper)		
392–94	Eugenius (usurper)	395–408	Arcadius
395–423	Honorius (395–408 Stilicho as regent)		
421	Constantius III	408–50	Theodosius II
423–25	Iohannes (usurper)	450–57	Marcian
425–55	Valentinian III	457–74	Leo
455	Petronius Maximus	474–91	Zeno
455–56	Avitus	(475–76	Basiliscus)
457–61	Majorian		
461–65	Libius Severus		
467–72	Anthemius		
472	Olybrius		
473	Glycerius		
473–75	Nepos		
475–76	Romulus Augustulus		

Barbarian rulers of Italy

476–93	Odoacer	491–518	Anastasius
493–526	Theoderic	518–27	Justin
526–34	Athalaric	527–65	Justinian
534–36	Theodahad		

name, Caesar. Thereafter, both Augustus and Caesar became titles meaning emperor.

The Latin word *imperator* (emperor)—originally a title that was given to a successful military commander—also came into use at this time. Emperors had other formal titles that appeared on coins, inscriptions, and public announcements, such as *Pater Patriae* ("Father of the Country") and *Princeps* ("First Citizen").

The good, the bad, and the mad

Some emperors ruled their people well and continued to develop the Roman state. Hadrian, for example, journeyed around the empire, organizing large-scale rebuilding in each province.

Other emperors, however, were cruel and murdered their rivals and opponents or they wasted public money. Some of them, according to Roman writers, were even dangerously mad. The emperor Gaius Caligula, for instance, was said to have planned to make his favorite horse a consul.

▲ This mosaic picture is of the emperor Justinian. He reconquered much of the western empire, which had been taken over by the Vandals in Africa, the Ostrogoths in Italy, and the Visigoths in Spain. The lands were gradually lost again.

Roman Religion

THE EARLY ROMANS BELIEVED THAT gods, goddesses, and powerful spirits were everywhere and that they controlled human actions. Gods and spirits might be friendly if offerings and prayers were made to them. This could take place in temples, at roadside or household altars, or at various other sacred places. The offerings included honey cakes, fruit, and wine poured out on the ground. Often animals were sacrificed in order to please the gods.

Gods and goddesses

As time went on, the Romans adopted gods and goddesses from other peoples, especially the Etruscans and the Greeks. They thought of these beings as large-size humans and portrayed them in statues and paintings. Some gods were thought to be more important than others, but each had his or her own special responsibility.

The "king and queen" of the Roman deities were Jupiter (great god of the sky) and Juno (patron goddess of women). Others included: Minerva (wisdom, crafts, and industries), Venus (beauty and love), Mars (war), Vulcan (fire), Vesta (hearth and home), Mercury (merchants), and Janus (two-headed god of doorways). Many other gods and goddesses were worshiped throughout the Roman Empire.

Emperor worship

When Rome became an empire, emperors were considered to be gods too, and temples were built for their worship. Several emperors were worshiped as gods before they died.

▶ Worship of the god Mithras was brought to Rome in the first century C.E. Here Mithras is shown killing a bull, whose flowing blood was thought to be a source of life.

▶ Underground temple to Mithras in Rome. Mithraism was carried all over the empire by soldiers and merchants. It was a "men-only" religion.

▼ Circular temple in Rome dedicated to the god Hercules who was said to have performed one of his 12 labors here. It was built in the second century B.C.E. in the Greek style.

◀ A fourth-century C.E. mosaic floor from a villa in Dorset, Britain. The center-piece shows the head of Christ and the first two letters of his name in Greek: x (Ch) and p (r).

Ceremonies and temples

Worship of a god or goddess usually involved processions, sacrifices, and offerings at an altar. The *pontifex* (priest) conducted the ceremony. Fine temples were built in towns and cities for the important god and for the ones considered special by the townspeople. The emperor Hadrian completed a large temple in Rome called the Pantheon, dedicated to all the gods. This has a dome 148 feet (45 m) in both height and diameter, which is the largest ever built by preindustrial methods. The inside of the dome was meant to represent the heavens, and the opening at the top symbolized the sun.

People also built altars inside their houses at which they could make offerings to the gods who protected the household. There were other spirits to worship as well—the *Penates* were the spirits of the cupboard or pantry.

◀ This sculpture from the arch of Titus in Rome shows the destruction of the Jewish Temple in Jerusalem in 70 C.E., when the gold seven-branched candlestick (the menorah) was carried off.

▼ Every five years the Romans held a census. This began with a ceremony at which a bull, a ram, and a pig were killed as a sacrifice to the gods.

Foreign religions

The Romans also accepted gods and goddesses that were worshiped in countries they ruled, including the Egyptian goddess Isis and the Persian god Mithras. At the same time, they violently suppressed minority religions if they thought they might threaten the empire's stability. For example, they pulled down the Temple in Jerusalem following the Jewish Revolt of 66–70 C.E. They hunted down the Druids and persecuted members of the fast-growing new religion, Christianity, who refused to worship the emperor. After the conversion of the emperor Constantine to Christianity in 313 C.E., Christianity became the official religion of the Roman Empire.

The Roman Baths

AT LEAST ONE BATH HOUSE WAS CONSIDERED essential for any Roman town. Pompeii had three big baths which the public could use, and everyone used them. It was cheap to get in, and children had free entrance. The baths were important places for relaxing, seeing friends, or even holding business meetings.

From cold dip to sauna

Some baths, such as the Stabian Baths at Pompeii, had separate facilities for men and women. If not, there were special times set aside for each group. First you undressed (in the *apodyterium*) and left your clothes in a locker or on a shelf. From there you passed into the cold, unheated room called a *frigidarium* and had a cold dip. Next you went into a warm room, the *tepidarium*.

From there you passed into the *caldarium*, the really hot room full of steam, with hot dip baths and a warm fountain for washing. This was heated by means of a hypocaust—a hollow space under the floor into which hot air was blown. The steam sweated out the dirt, which could be scraped off using strigils (see below). A slave might do this for you and then massage you and oil your skin. There was also a *laconicum*, or sauna, to go through if you wanted intense dry heat.

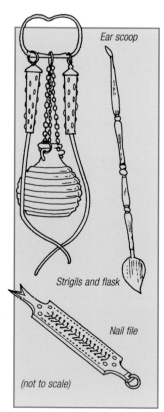

Ear scoop

Strigils and flask

Nail file

(not to scale)

▶ The Stabian Baths at Pompeii.
Men's baths: **1** dressing-room, **2** cold room, **3** warm room, **4** hot room, **5** sauna.
Women's baths: **6** dressing-room, **7** warm room, **8** hot room.
9 Furnaces. **10** Exercise yard.
11 Swimming pool.
12 Bathrooms.

◀ Instruments used at the baths. The curved bronze strigils were for scraping off the sweat and dirt. The flasks had a mixture of olive oil and pumice for cleaning and refreshing the skin.

Afterward you could go out into the open courtyard for exercise—perhaps a ball game or just a walk. At the baths there was also a small swimming pool and lavatories.

Working in the baths

Large numbers of slaves were needed in order to keep the baths going. The heat for the rooms and the water was produced in a furnace that blew hot air under the floors and up through the walls to the roof. Floors above hypocausts were raised on pillars. Other slaves carried out massage or brought towels to the visitors to the baths. Food sellers would also come in with trays of snacks or sweets.

Noisy place to live

"I live over the public baths—you know what that means. Ugh! It's sickening. First there are the 'strongmen' doing their exercises and swinging heavy lead weights about with grunts and groans. Next the lazy ones having a cheap massage—I can hear someone being slapped on the shoulders. Then there's the man who always likes the sound of his own voice in the bath. And what about the ones who leap into the pool making a huge splash!"— Lucius Seneca, in Rome about 63 C.E.

▼ The Great Bath at Bath, in southwest England. The Romans valued the excellent health-giving properties of the pure spring water they found here.

Imperial Rome

"I FOUND ROME BUILT OF SUN-DRIED BRICKS. I leave a city covered in marble." This is what the emperor Augustus is said to have boasted at the end of his reign.

The city of Rome, now with a population of more than 1 million, needed complete reorganization. Augustus was the first to carry out large-scale redevelopment and he did indeed transform the city. Augustus repaired the aqueducts and water systems and built roads, a theater, and a senate house. He repaired 82 temples and built several new ones.

Two great fires

During the reign of the emperor Nero a serious fire swept through Rome. The historian Tacitus tells us that in this disaster of 64 C.E. only four of Rome's 14 districts survived. Some were destroyed to ground level; in others only a few houses survived.

Nero began to rebuild the city to include an enormous palace for himself. We are told by the writer Suetonius that the Golden House, as it was called, stood in a great park, and that parts of the building were covered in gold. When it was finished, Nero—who has a reputation for being a vain and foolish man—is reported to have said: "Good, now I can live like a human being at last!"

▼ The arch pictured below, built in 203 C.E., commemorates the triumphs of the emperor Septimius Severus and his sons over the Parthians and Arabs.

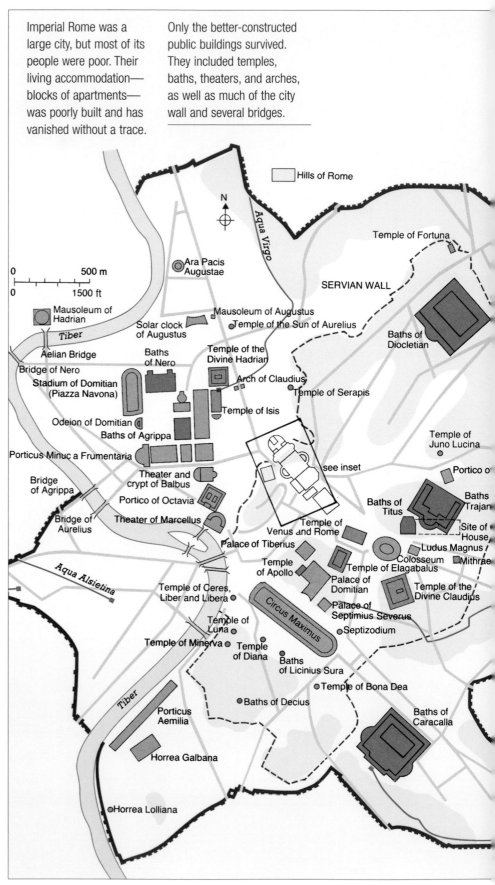

Imperial Rome was a large city, but most of its people were poor. Their living accommodation—blocks of apartments—was poorly built and has vanished without a trace.

Only the better-constructed public buildings survived. They included temples, baths, theaters, and arches, as well as much of the city wall and several bridges.

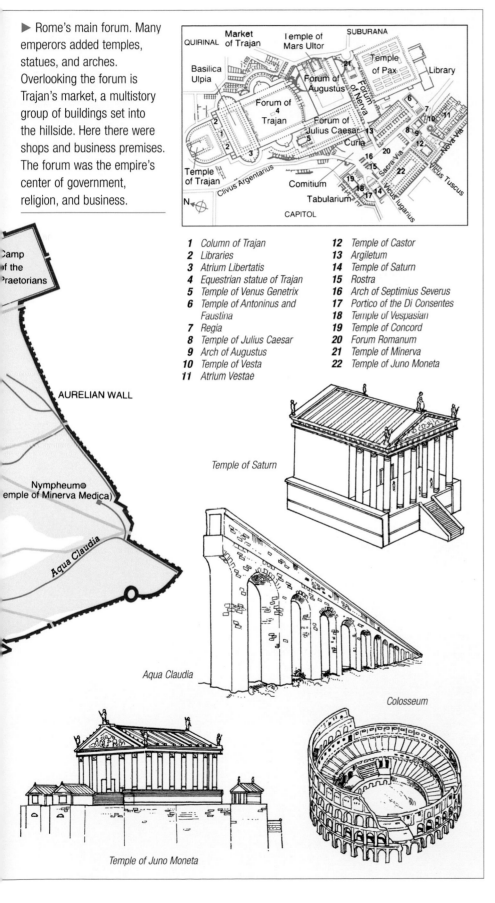

► Rome's main forum. Many emperors added temples, statues, and arches. Overlooking the forum is Trajan's market, a multistory group of buildings set into the hillside. Here there were shops and business premises. The forum was the empire's center of government, religion, and business.

1	Column of Trajan	**12**	Temple of Castor
2	Libraries	**13**	Argiletum
3	Atrium Libertatis	**14**	Temple of Saturn
4	Equestrian statue of Trajan	**15**	Rostra
5	Temple of Venus Genetrix	**16**	Arch of Septimius Severus
6	Temple of Antoninus and Faustina	**17**	Portico of the Di Consentes
7	Regia	**18**	Temple of Vespasian
8	Temple of Julius Caesar	**19**	Temple of Concord
9	Arch of Augustus	**20**	Forum Romanum
10	Temple of Vesta	**21**	Temple of Minerva
11	Atrium Vestae	**22**	Temple of Juno Moneta

Temple of Saturn

Aqua Claudia

Colosseum

Temple of Juno Moneta

Nero's Golden House was destroyed by another fire in 104 C.E. Only his colossal statue, which stood in the entrance hall, survived. It gave its name to the amphitheater that was later built close by: the Colosseum. On part of the site of Nero's palace the emperor Trajan built his baths, the first of three great bath complexes.

Aqueducts and baths

It was not only Augustus and Nero who carried out grand building schemes. In 52 C.E. the emperor Claudius completed a large aqueduct that had been started by Caligula. This aqueduct, called Aqua Claudia, brought water to Rome from a source 40 miles (64 km) away.

Large amounts of water were needed for the huge baths that several emperors had built. The three largest groups of baths were those of Trajan, Caracalla, and Diocletian.

Forum and temples

The greatest changes since republican times were probably in the city center around the main forum. The forum, or open square, was where the business of the city was carried out. Around it, buildings called basilicas were used as law courts, to hold meetings, and to conduct business.

In imperial Rome the forum became so important for ceremonies and religion that it was no longer used as a marketplace. Other markets were built for particular goods, such as the *forum boarium* (cattle market) near the Circus Maximus.

Many temples were also built. The temple of Saturn stood on the edge of the forum. The temple of Venus and Roma was built in 135 C.E. near Nero's ruined palace.

The temple of Juno Moneta towered above, on a nearby hill. "Moneta" (from the Latin *monere*, meaning to warn) meant that Juno warned the Romans of an enemy approaching. The temple later became a place for minting coins. Our word "money" comes from this Latin word.

On the outskirts of town

Despite these magnificent public buildings, the poor people of Rome lived in appalling slums. By the third century C.E. the city had expanded so much that a new wall was needed to encircle and defend it. For the first time in Rome's history this new Aurelian Wall went around the camp of the army unit that provided the emperor with his defense.

Arena and Stadium

ALL OVER THE EMPIRE, ROMANS ENJOYED plays and concerts at the theater, chariot-racing at the stadium, and bloody sports at the amphitheater. Going to the amphitheater was probably the most popular activity. These oval-shaped buildings could hold huge crowds, often the entire population of a town. People would spend the whole day there.

Gladiators in combat

Various kinds of combat were staged in the amphitheater. Most popular were the bouts between fighters, called gladiators, who fought with each other in fierce combat to the death. Rich people and politicians paid for schools of gladiators to arrange the bouts for their entertainment. The gladiators were armed in different ways to make the fights more interesting. There were gladiators completely covered with armor, others fighting with just a sword and shield, and some, called *retiarii*, who fought with a net and three-pronged spear.

Gladiators were usually slaves or war captives. The prize for those who fought well and succeeded in entertaining the crowd might be their freedom. Convicted criminals were also made to fight in the amphitheater while the crowd looked on. At lunchtime there was usually a chance to see them fight to the death. The last one left alive was brought back to fight again the next day.

Man against beast

Wild animals—such as lions, bears, snakes, deer, and even elephants—would be fought by gladiators in the arena. Huge numbers of them were imported from the provinces, especially after some species had become extinct in Italy.

Amphitheaters were sometimes flooded in order to recreate sea battles, complete with crocodiles to eat those who fell overboard. Not all Romans were entertained by combat and death, however. In the first century B.C.E. the philosopher Cicero wrote:

"What pleasure can it give a person of taste when either a feeble human being is torn to pieces by an incredibly strong wild animal or a handsome beast is transfixed by a spear?"

Chariot-racing

An exciting and dangerous sport enjoyed by many thousands of Romans was chariot-racing. Many towns had a stadium in which four teams—wearing red, blue, green, and white colors—all raced around a central barrier.

In the biggest stadium of all, the Circus Maximus in Rome, those charioteers who survived the race had traveled about 4 miles (6 km) during their seven laps of the enormous stadium. Some of the charioteers became idols of the crowd and earned huge sums of money as a result.

▲ This model of ancient Rome shows the Circus Maximus and the Colosseum (top right).

◄ This ampitheater at El Djem in North Africa was the third largest in the empire.

► The games were public shows that involved danger and excitement, as in chariot races (far right). Gladiatorial combats resulted in blood-letting, in front of as many as 50,000 people.

The Later Empire

F OR MUCH OF THE THIRD CENTURY C.E. there was unrest in the Roman Empire. There were raids along all the frontiers. Forts had to be built on the coasts of Britain and northern Gaul. Between 235 and 284 C.E. there were more than 18 emperors, each lasting only a few years before they were murdered or expelled.

The legions elect Diocletian

One of the most important changes in the history of the Roman Empire took place in 284 C.E. Diocletian, born in the province of Dalmatia, was the commander of Emperor Numerian's bodyguard. When Numerian was murdered, the army chose Diocletian to succeed him as emperor.

Reorganization of empire and army

Diocletian's main reform was to divide the huge empire into two. He ruled the east from Nicomedia in Bithynia. He chose an old friend, Maximian, to be emperor in the west, ruling from Rome. In 293 C.E. he established what was known as "four-man" rule by appointing two successors, one to help each emperor. The arrangement worked, and Diocletian did not need to visit Rome until 10 years later.

The empire was reorganized into 12 districts called dioceses. Each had a governor called a *vicarius*. The army was enlarged at this time. The legions were also reorganized into permanent frontier troops and small mobile units that could be moved quickly to wherever they were needed.

Diocletian issued an official list of prices for goods, which had to be followed throughout the empire. To charge more meant death or exile.

▲ Part of a mosaic outside the offices of shipping firms at the port of Ostia. Dolphins were a favorite sea design. In the background a lighthouse can be seen.

► Diocletian's empire. "Four-man" rule brought stability to Roman lands.

▼ Tomb painting of a ferry boat loaded with grain at Ostia. The captain (*magister*) is called Farnaces, and the ship the *Isis Giminiana*.

► Bust of the emperor Diocletian, found at his capital city, Nicomedia.

1 GERMANIA I
2 NARBONENSIS II
3 VIENNENSIS
4 ALPES MARITIMAE
5 ALPES COTTIAE
6 VENETIA AND HISTRIA
7 VALERIA
8 DACIA MEDITERRANEA
9 AUGUSTA EUPHRATENSIS
Scale 1:15 000 000

0   1000 km
0   600 mile

The reforms of Diocletian

211 C.E. The emperor Septimius Severus dies in York. There are now about 46 provinces in the empire, but many are later subdivided.

284 C.E. Diocletian declared emperor.

286 C.E. Maximian made emperor in the west.

293 C.E. Diocletian creates a "rule of four men": two emperors rule alongside two successors.

296 C.E. Diocletian reorganizes the empire's finances. Prices are fixed for coins of gold, silver, and bronze. From now on all minting is done by the state. New tax system introduced.

301 C.E. Diocletian issues official list of prices for goods throughout the empire. But the system is abandoned as unworkable.

303 C.E. In ill health Diocletian gives up the throne.

313 C.E. Diocletian dies.

314 C.E. The empire now has 101 provinces.

330 C.E. The emperor Constantine the Great moves the capital of a reunited Roman Empire to Constantinople.

Diocletian dioceses
- Hispaniae
- Viennensis
- Galliae
- Britanniae
- Italia
- Pannoniae
- Moesiae
- Thraciae
- Asiana
- Pontica
- Oriens
- Africa

— Severan province boundary
— Diocletian province boundary
CARIA Diocletian province name
♦ Principal Roman mint

The Roman Ship

EVERYONE LIVING IN THE ROMAN WORLD relied on food and other goods carried to them by ship. Large quantities of food, such as wheat, could be transported more easily by ship than across land. By the second century C.E. routes had been established all over the Roman Empire.

Luxury goods came to Rome and other towns from as far away as India and China.

"The arrival and departure of ships never stops—it is amazing that the sea, not to mention the harbor, is big enough for these merchant ships."—Aelius Aristides.

Ostia—the port of Rome

As the capital of the empire, Rome needed a harbor by the sea. The emperor Claudius constructed an artificial harbor near the port of Ostia at the mouth of the Tiber River to cope with the enormous volume of trade. In 103 C.E., 50 years later, the emperor Trajan made this harbor even bigger and connected it to Ostia by a deep channel.

In the second century C.E. about 50,000 people lived and worked in Ostia. Private firms carried out most of the trade in the port and built great warehouses as well as smart offices.

▲ A ship is about to dock. This scene, carved in marble in about 200 C.E., was found near Trajan's harbor. The flaming lighthouse seen behind the ship is probably the one recorded as built by the emperor Claudius.

▼ This merchant ship could have carried about 6,000 amphorae (flasks). The oars at the back are for steering the ship. The large wooden goose's head represents the Egyptian goddess Isis, the seafarer's guardian.

▼ A ship unloading its cargo of wine, oil, wheat, and cloth at Ostia. Much of the wheat would be used as free dole for the 200,000 people of Rome who were unemployed or very poor.

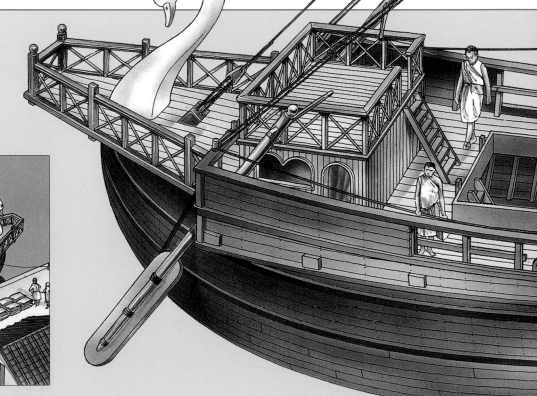

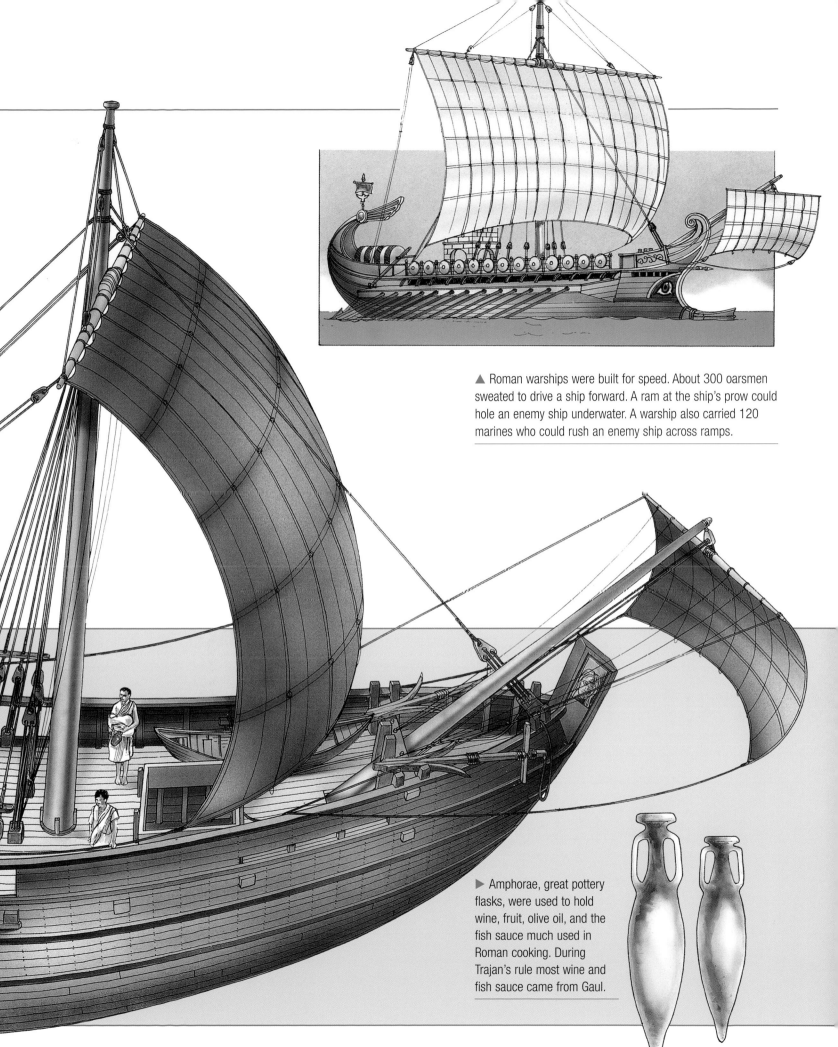

▲ Roman warships were built for speed. About 300 oarsmen sweated to drive a ship forward. A ram at the ship's prow could hole an enemy ship underwater. A warship also carried 120 marines who could rush an enemy ship across ramps.

▶ Amphorae, great pottery flasks, were used to hold wine, fruit, olive oil, and the fish sauce much used in Roman cooking. During Trajan's rule most wine and fish sauce came from Gaul.

Part Two

The Geography of an Empire

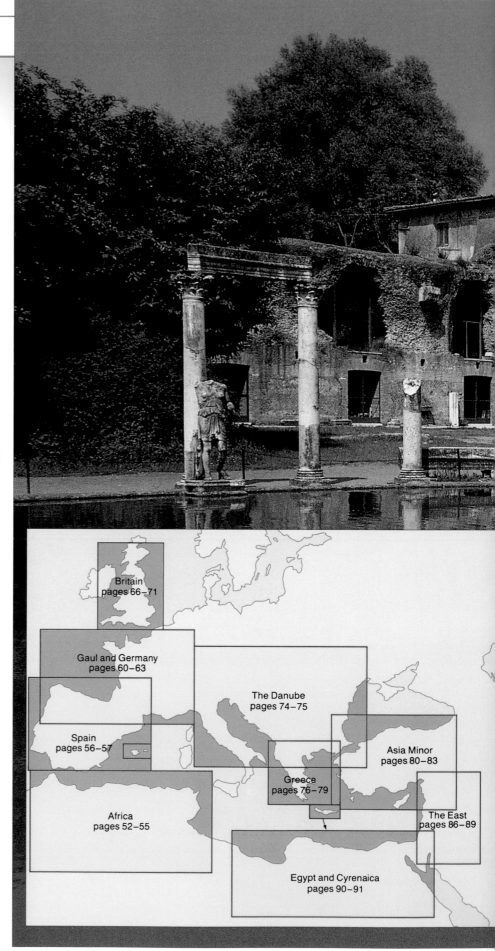

▲ A wealthy Roman woman, about 50 B.C.E.

▶ Hadrian's villa near Rome, 125–135 C.E.

Inset Key to maps in this section of the book.

Africa

THE ROMANS BEGAN TO RULE THE province of Africa in 146 B.C.E., after the destruction of Carthage. At first the province consisted of the land we now know as Tunisia. Later Roman territory stretched as far as Libya to the east and Morocco to the west. Mountains and deserts formed its southern borders.

Exporting to the empire

This was a very rich part of the Roman world. At one time it supplied two-thirds of Rome's corn supply. The province's olives and olive oil were exported to other parts of the Roman Empire. Archaeologists have found olive presses and great storage jars sunk into the ground in many African villas.

Africa also supplied wild animals for the amphitheaters of the empire. North African leopards, wild asses, rhinos, lions, elephants, antelopes, zebra, giraffes, and ostriches were "hunted" and killed as part of the public games in many Roman cities.

It was the Roman army that was responsible for making Africa a prosperous part of the empire. About

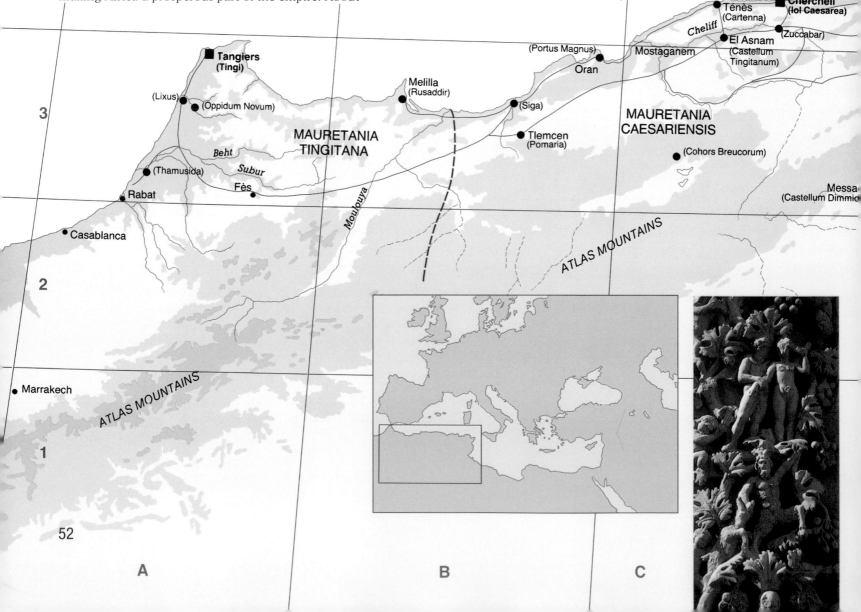

◀ The water source for Carthage was more than 30 miles (50 km) away, so an aqueduct had to be built to carry the water. Water was stored in huge cisterns in the city.

▶ This colorful mosaic decorated a town house in Thugga (now called Dougga). The man is fishing with much the same equipment as we use today: a rod, a landing net, and even a basket for the catch.

28,000 troops patrolled this region from their network of forts and camps. Soldiers built roads and surveyed the countryside. The land was divided into regular plots, and great farming estates were created. Many of these estates were owned by the emperor or by wealthy people living in far-off Rome.

New colonies

There had been a number of towns on the North African coast before the Romans arrived. Carthage had been Hannibal's capital city. In the west, in Mauretania, the emperor Augustus established 12 new colonies for retired soldiers and their families.

These new townspeople soon helped build a Roman way of life on the southern shores of the Mediterranean. But the people who originally lived in this part of North Africa still kept their language and some of their own customs.

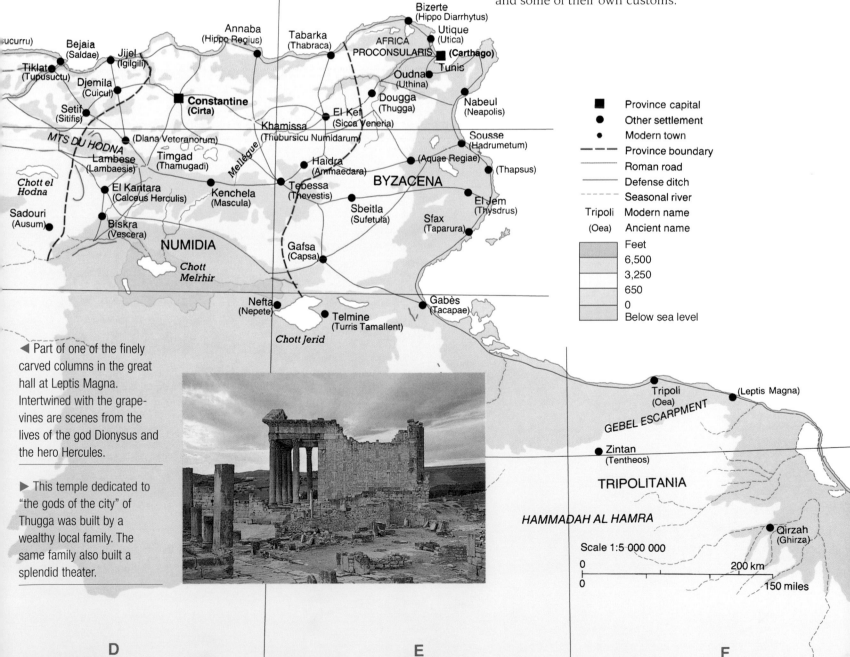

◀ Part of one of the finely carved columns in the great hall at Leptis Magna. Intertwined with the grapevines are scenes from the lives of the god Dionysus and the hero Hercules.

▶ This temple dedicated to "the gods of the city" of Thugga was built by a wealthy local family. The same family also built a splendid theater.

Map labels

ucurru)
Bejaia (Saldae)
Jijel (Igilgili)
Tiklat (Tupusuctu)
Djemila (Cuicul)
Setif (Sitifis)
MTS DU HODNA
Lambese (Lambaesis)
Chott el Hodna
El Kantara (Calceus Herculis)
Sadouri (Ausum)
Biskra (Vescera)
NUMIDIA
Chott Melrhir

Annaba (Hippo Regius)
Constantine (Cirta)
(Diana Veteranorum)
Timgad (Thamugadi)
Mellègue
Kenchela (Mascula)
Tebessa (Thevestis)
Gafsa (Capsa)

Tabarka (Thabraca)
Khamissa (Thubursicu Numidarum)
El Kef (Sicca Veneria)
Haidra (Ammaedara)
Sbeitla (Sufetula)
Nefta (Nepete)
Telmine (Turris Tamallent)
Chott Jerid

Bizerte (Hippo Diarrhytus)
AFRICA PROCONSULARIS
Utique (Utica)
■ (Carthago)
Tunis
Oudna (Uthina)
Dougga (Thugga)
Nabeul (Neapolis)
Sousse (Hadrumetum)
(Aquae Regiae)
(Thapsus)
BYZACENA
El Jem (Thysdrus)
Sfax (Taparura)
Gabès (Tacapae)

Tripoli (Oea)
(Leptis Magna)
GEBEL ESCARPMENT
Zintan (Tentheos)
TRIPOLITANIA
HAMMADAH AL HAMRA
Qirzah (Ghirza)

Legend

■ Province capital
● Other settlement
• Modern town
– – – Province boundary
—— Roman road
—— Defense ditch
- - - Seasonal river
Tripoli Modern name
(Oea) Ancient name

Feet
6,500
3,250
650
0
Below sea level

Scale 1:5 000 000
0 ___ 200 km
0 ___ 150 miles

D   E   F

Africa • Sites

Leptis Magna

FOUNDED POSSIBLY AS EARLY AS THE fifth century B.C.E., the town of Leptis Magna in North Africa was laid out near the harbor, which was well protected from the open sea. The central part of the Roman Empire was far away to the north, but Leptis was connected to it through trade. A lighthouse and a beacon marked the harbor entrance for ships. Produce such as corn and olive oil was exported from here.

Fine buildings

Wealthy from trade and agriculture, the rich citizens of Leptis put up magnificent buildings for the townspeople to use. The emperor Septimius Severus, who came from Leptis, provided the town with a new

▲ An inscribed milestone from Leptis Magna.

▼ In 1 C.E. this theater was built in Leptis by a rich nobleman. The columns on the right are part of a temple.

harbor, a colonnaded forum, and an aisled basilica. An imposing street with columns on each side built during the reign of the emperor Hadrian ran from the harbor to the public baths. Leptis Magna became the third most important city in Africa after Carthage and Alexandria.

The emperor Septimius revisited his birthplace in 203 C.E. To mark the occasion the townspeople erected a great memorial arch at a crossroads, which could be seen from all directions.

Today you can stand at the back of the town's theater and look out over the Mediterranean. We can still see a lot of ancient Leptis because its remains were preserved under sand dunes that gradually engulfed the town.

Timgad

UNLIKE LEPTIS, WHICH WAS ORIGINALLY founded by the Phoenicians, Timgad was a Roman new town. In 100 C.E. it was established as a colony for retired soldiers of the Third Legion, which was stationed at Lambaesis close by. Timgad lies at the edge of the desert near the Aurès Mountains in present-day Algeria. Like many Roman colonies, it was laid out almost exactly square, like an army fort. Each side was about 385 yards (350 m) long.

Timgad was divided into regular blocks (called *insulae*) in the Roman fashion. The town had 111 blocks, each of about the same size. This type of town planning helped the early settlers build a well-organized town. It also made it easy for government officials and citizens to find their way through the paved streets. Roman forts were similarly laid out.

Most of the town was taken up with houses for the newly settled army veterans and their families. The original planners did not leave much room for public buildings. You can see the forum and the theater on the aerial photograph. They are built close to the junction of the two main streets, the center of town. There was also a market and a bath building.

Growth and success

To provide all the amenities the citizens wanted, and to house a growing population, Timgad's planners gradually had to begin building outside the original square site.

These new amenities, which date from the mid-second century C.E., included another 13 baths, a library, temples, another market just for clothes, and a triumphal arch. Scratched on the steps of a public lavatory was a gaming board with the words "to hunt, to bathe, to play, to laugh, that is to live."

As the town's population grew, the town council also allowed houses to be built outside the original area. The wall which had at first surrounded the town was taken down, and suburbs grew up to the west and the north. You can see at the top of the photograph the buildings beyond the wall—no longer following the regular military-style layout.

Timgad's large and thriving population helped bring peace to this frontier area. The rich farming countryside around Timgad provided the wealth for it to develop.

▶ This photograph of Timgad taken from the air shows the town's strictly regular plan. The shadows of the rows of columns that lined the two main streets can just be seen.

▼ Timgad's main street. It led to the legionary fort of Lambaesis. A great deal of money went into providing towns with stone-paved roads and colonnaded arcades.

Spain and Portugal

EARLY ROMAN SETTLEMENTS IN SPAIN were in the south and east. When the emperor Augustus conquered the whole of the Iberian peninsula he divided it into three provinces. It quickly became "romanized," although one army legion remained on duty in the Basque territory in the north in case of rebellion.

Roman Spain's oldest and most famous town was Italica, birthplace of the emperors Trajan and Hadrian. It was founded in 206 B.C.E. as a place of settlement for soldiers wounded in the battle of Illipa. During Hadrian's reign it was redesigned with colonnaded streets and a large amphitheater.

Mines, wine, and fish sauce

"Almost all of Spain has mines producing lead, iron, tin, silver, and gold," noted the Roman writer Pliny in the first century C.E. There were also copper mines. The Roman authorities believed that their provinces should produce wealth for the state, and the state owned most of the Spanish mines.

As well as mining, Spain exported huge quantities of olive oil and wine. It was also famous throughout the empire for its salted fish sauce, called *garum*, which was exported widely and came to be used in many Roman recipes.

▼ This stone aqueduct brought water to the city of Segovia from Riofrio 10 miles (16 km) away. Its arches stretched nearly 1 mile (1.6 km) to carry the water across the city. At the very top, it was 100 ft (30 m) above the ground.

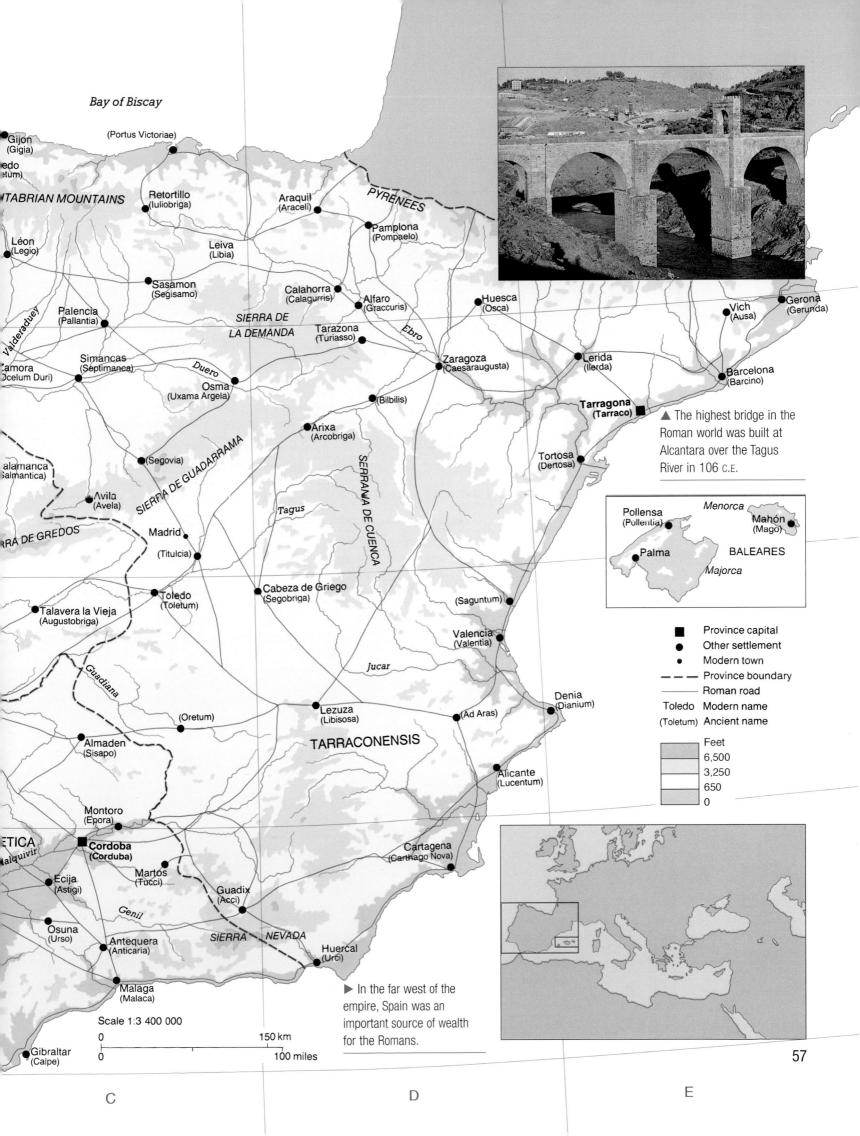

Bay of Biscay

Gijon
(Gigia)

(Portus Victoriae)

edo
(etum)

CANTABRIAN MOUNTAINS

Retortillo
(Iuliobriga)

Araquil
(Araceli)

PYRENEES

Léon
(Legio)

Leiva
(Libia)

Pamplona
(Pompaelo)

Sasamon
(Segisamo)

Calahorra
(Calagurris)

Alfaro
(Graccuris)

Huesca
(Osca)

Vich
(Ausa)

Gerona
(Gerunda)

Palencia
(Pallantia)

SIERRA DE
LA DEMANDA

Tarazona
(Turiasso)

Ebro

Zaragoza
(Caesaraugusta)

Lerida
(Ilerda)

Valderaduey

Simancas
(Septimanca)

Duero

Barcelona
(Barcino)

amora
Ocelum Duri)

Osma
(Uxama Argela)

(Bilbilis)

Tarragona
(Tarraco)

▲ The highest bridge in the
Roman world was built at
Alcantara over the Tagus
River in 106 C.E.

alamanca
almantica)

(Segovia)

SIERRA DE GUADARRAMA

Arixa
(Arcobriga)

Tortosa
(Dertosa)

Ávila
(Avela)

Pollensa
(Pollentia)

Menorca

Mahón
(Mago)

RRA DE GREDOS

Tagus

SERRANÍA DE CUENCA

Palma

BALEARES

Madrid
(Titulcia)

Majorca

Toledo
(Toletum)

Cabeza de Griego
(Segobriga)

(Saguntum)

■ Province capital
● Other settlement
• Modern town
--- Province boundary
— Roman road
Toledo Modern name
(Toletum) Ancient name

Talavera la Vieja
(Augustobriga)

Valencia
(Valentia)

Guadiana

Jucar

Denia
(Dianium)

Feet
6,500
3,250
650
0

Lezuza
(Libisosa)

(Oretum)

(Ad Aras)

Almaden
(Sisapo)

TARRACONENSIS

Alicante
(Lucentum)

Montoro
(Epora)

ETICA

Cordoba
(Corduba)

Cartagena
(Carthago Nova)

alquivir

Ecija
(Astigi)

Martos
(Tucci)

Guadix
(Acci)

Osuna
(Urso)

Genil

Antequera
(Anticaria)

SIERRA NEVADA

Huercal
(Urci)

▶ In the far west of the
empire, Spain was an
important source of wealth
for the Romans.

Malaga
(Malaca)

Scale 1:3 400 000

0   150 km

0   100 miles

Gibraltar
(Calpe)

57

C   D   E

The Roman Town

IN 331 C.E. THE PEOPLE OF ORCISTUS IN GALATIA asked the emperor Constantine to grant them the status of a town. The emperor replied:

"They have declared that in the past their village had all the splendors of a town, appointed officials each year and was filled with people and citizens. Many public roads led to it, there is an adequate supply of water, public and private baths and it is adorned with statues."

Anyone traveling through the Roman Empire would expect to see all towns with much the same facilities for their inhabitants. Early Roman towns developed gradually from earlier foundations, Etruscan or Greek perhaps. In the provinces many completely new towns were established on land that had not been built on before.

The town plan
What made up a Roman town? If it was a new town, or if part of an old one was rebuilt, there would be properly laid-out streets crossing at right angles. These divided the town into regular blocks, known as *insulae* (islands).

If the town was rich enough and was given permission by Rome, it might build a stone wall around itself as protection. The streets would be paved if possible. Outside the town's limits would be the cemeteries.

Water and sewage
Aqueducts brought fresh water into the town. It was distributed by underground pipes and by fountains. Public lavatories were provided, usually as part of the public baths. Sewage and waste water (especially from baths) would also be dealt with in the town's plan. Officials were appointed specifically to look after these services.

Public buildings
Most of the town would be taken up with houses, shops, and workshops. The most important public area was the forum, the town square. This was where markets were held and business was conducted. Around it there would be law courts, council offices, public halls (basilicas), and temples.

If the town was wealthy there might be a theater and perhaps an amphitheater as well. In addition, there had to be public baths, since no town was considered civilized without them.

▼ The Roman town Herculaneum is close to Pompeii on the Bay of Naples. It was made uninhabitable by the eruption of Mount Vesuvius in 79 C.E. Dating back to the sixth century B.C.E., it is said to have been founded by the hero-god Hercules.

The small coastal town had around 5,000 inhabitants. It had some elegant houses of two or three stories with gardens and sea views. Many of the ordinary houses had shops or workshops on the ground floor. Not all the town has been excavated, but the forum, a basilica, a theater, a public bath house, a gymnasium, and a swimming pool have been found.

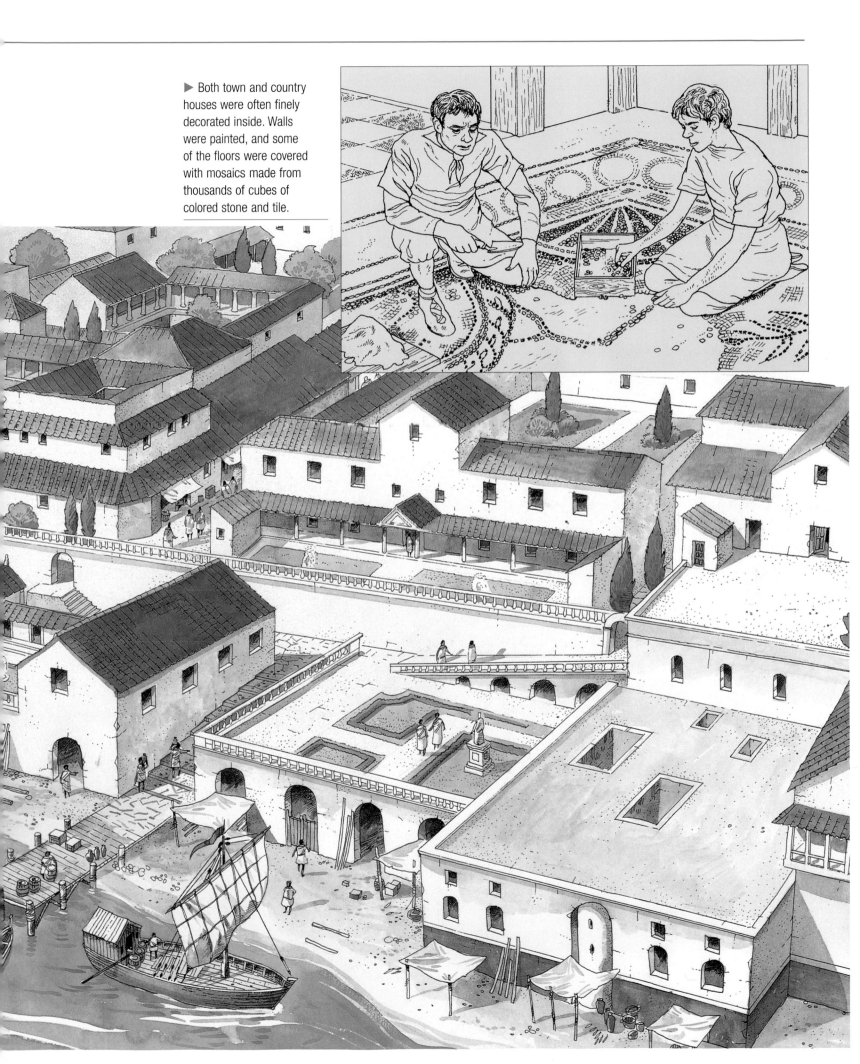

► Both town and country houses were often finely decorated inside. Walls were painted, and some of the floors were covered with mosaics made from thousands of cubes of colored stone and tile.

Gaul and Germany

IN THE AREAS OF GALLIA AND GERMANIA lived a number of Celtic-speaking peoples. Ammianus Marcellinus wrote, "Nearly all the Gauls are tall, fair-haired, and have a ruddy complexion. They are always quarreling and are proud and insolent." In the far south of Gallia some settlements, such as Massilia (Marseille), had been established as early as 600 B.C.E. by the Greeks. Later Julius Caesar conquered a vast area to the north and created new boundaries for the Roman world in the west, as far as the Atlantic seaboard. It was from northern Gallia that Caesar launched the first invasion of Britain in 55 B.C.E.

"Long-haired Gaul"

This new area can be divided into three very different parts. In the south the earlier settlements were enlarged and "romanized." Magnificent Roman remains can still be seen in towns such as Nîmes, Arles, and Orange. The biggest of the towns in the area was Lyon, and at Narbonne on the Mediterranean coast a large port was established.

In the north and west, which the Romans called Gallia Comata ("long-haired Gaul"), the land was open and fertile. Large farming estates filled the well-populated countryside. In Germania, near to the Rhine River, new colonies (towns for retired soldiers) were built as well as a line of forts to form a new frontier.

In the late empire the balance of trading power shifted from the south to the north. This was largely due to an imperial court at Trier (Augusta Treverorum), attracting increased financial and material resources.

▶ Many places specialized in particular crafts and exported to the rest of the empire. This fine-quality glass jug comes from Urdingen.

▼ One of the impressive main gateways in the city walls of Autun. This entrance has two arches for vehicles and two for pedestrians.

◀ Bronze statue of a farmworker found in Trier. The cloak and woolen leggings provided warmth in the northern winter.

■	Province capital
●	Other settlement
– – –	Province boundary
———	Roman road
Paris	Modern name
(Lutetia)	Ancient name
⋈	Mountain pass

	Feet
	6,500
	4,900
	1,300
	650
	0
	Below sea level

▶ The Alps comprise a barrier dividing France from Italy. The Romans would talk about "this side" (their side) or "the other side" of the Alps. In France the earliest Roman towns were in "the Province"—today called Provence.

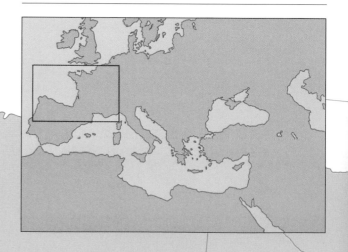

6

5

Valkenburg

GERMANIA
INFERIOR

Nijmegen
(Noviomagus)

Xanten
(Vetera)

Boulogne
(Gesoriacum)

Tongeren
(Atuatuca)

Neuss
(Novaesium)

Köln
(Colonia Agrippina)

Bonn
(Bonna)

Koblenz
(Confluentes)

TAURUS
MTS

Tournai
(Turnacum)

Schelde

Meuse

Wiesbaden
(Aquae Mattiacae)

Mainz (Moguntiacum)

English Channel

Cambrai
(Camaracum)

Amiens
(Samarobriva)

Nizy
(Minatiacum)

Arlon
(Orolaunum)

Trier
(Augusta Treverorum)

Mosel

Worms
(Borbetomagus)

4

Estrées–sur–Noye

BELGICA

Cherbourg
(Coriallum)

Rouen
(Rotomagus)

Beauvais
(Caesaromagus)

Speyer
(Noviomagus)

Bayeux
(Augustodurum)

Lisieux
(Noviomagus)

Seine

Reims (Durocortorum)

Metz (Divodurum)

Toul
(Tullum)

Strasbourg
(Argentorate)

Baden-Baden
(Aquae)

Paris
(Lutetia)

Marne

Seine

Neckar

Avranches
(Legedia)

Sées
(Seii)

Chartres
(Autricum)

Troyes
(Augustobona)

Nijon
(Noviomagus)

VOSGES MTS

Rhine

BLACK
FOREST

Rennes
(Condate)

LUGDUNENSIS

Sens
(Agedincum)

Le Mans
(Suindinum)

Angers
(Iuliomagus)

Tours
(Caesarodunum)

GERMANIA
SUPERIOR

Augst
(Augusta Rauricorum)

Windisch
(Vindonissa)

Nantes
(Portus Namnetum)

Dijon
(Dibio)

Besançon (Besontio)

3

Bressuire
(Segora)

Bourges
(Avaricum)

Autun
(Augustodunum)

Chalon–sur–Saône
(Cavillonum)

L de Neuchâtel

Saône

JURA
MTS

Vevey (Viviscus)

ALPS

Poitiers
(Limonum)

Argenton
(Argentomagus)

Nyons
(Noviodunum)

L Léman

ALPES GRAIAE
ET POENINAE

Rom
(Rauranum)

Néris-les-Bains
(Aquae Neri)

Geneva

Royan
(Noviorigum)

Vienne

Limoges
(Augustoritum)

Clermont-Ferrand
(Augustonemetum)

Lyon
(Lugdunum)

Feurs
(Forum Segusiavorcum)

Rhône

Aime
(Axima)

Angoulême
(Iculisma)

AQUITANIA

MASSIF
CENTRAL

Vienne
(Vienna)

Moutiers
(Darantasia)

2

Allier

Grenoble
(Culuro)

Isère

Susa
(Segusio)

Périgueux
(Vesunna)

Bordeaux
(Burdigala)

Dordogne

Cahors
(Divona)

Lot

Rhône

NARBONENSIS

Embrun
(Eburodurum)

ALPES
COTTIAE

Garonne

Bazas
(Vasates)

Agen (Aginnum)

Rodez
(Segodunum)

Tarn

Uzès
(Ucetia)

Orange
(Arausio)

Digne
(Dinia)

ALPES
MARITIMAE

Adour

Lectoure
(Lactora)

Toulouse
(Tolosa)

Lodève
(Luteva)

Nîmes
(Nemausus)

St.Rémy
(Glanum)

Durance

Cimiez
(Cemenelum)

Bayonne
(Lapurdum)

Auch
(Elimberris)

Arles
(Arelate)

Aix-en-Provence
(Aquae Sextiae)

Antibes
(Antipolis)

Béziers
(Baeterrae)

Marseille
(Massilia)

Fréjus
(Forum Iulii)

1

PYRENEES

Carcassonne
(Carcaso)

Narbonne
(Narbo)

Castel Roussillon
(Ruscino)

Mediterranean Sea

Scale 1:4 000 000

150 km

100 miles

A   B   C   D

Villa at Estrées-sur-Noye

THE AERIAL PHOTOGRAPH AND DRAWING show a villa, or farming estate, at Estrées-sur-Noye in the valley of the Somme River in northern France. It is not far from the town of Amiens, which the Romans called Samarobriva in the province of Gallia. This area has been much surveyed by archaeologists in recent years, mainly from the air, and more than 1,000 villas have been discovered there.

The land must have been fertile and well farmed in the Roman period. The villa at Estrées-sur-Noye is like many others found in the same area. Its farm buildings are contained in a walled courtyard that measures 385 yards (350 m) in length. On the photograph a rectangle can be seen near the main gateway. This was probably the site of a small shrine used by the farmworkers.

▶ You can see the outline of the buildings clearly because stone and mortar from the walls have been brought to the surface by deep plowing.

▼ A reconstruction of the villa. Notice that the owner's house is set in its own walled garden. The other buildings are for workers and animals, and for storing farm produce and machinery.

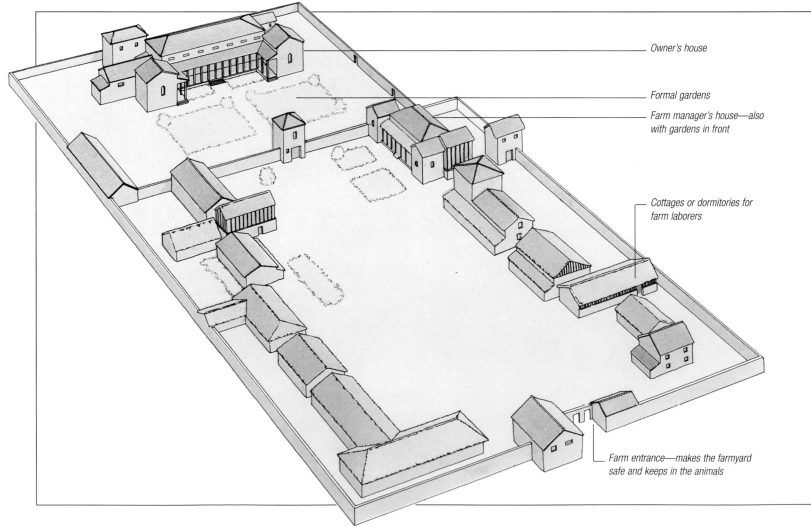

Owner's house

Formal gardens

Farm manager's house—also with gardens in front

Cottages or dormitories for farm laborers

Farm entrance—makes the farmyard safe and keeps in the animals

Buildings at Nîmes | City at Trier

THE ROMAN CITY OF NEMAUSUS LIES under the modern city of Nîmes in Provence, southern France. It was first a Celtic and then a Greek settlement. The walled Roman city was laid out in 16 B.C.E. especially for retired soldiers. In an area that specialized in exporting its quality farm produce it became a very rich city, with a population of about 50,000 in the second century C.E. The city is famous today for its Roman remains—the amphitheater below, the aqueduct called Pont du Gard, and the temple called Maison Carrée.

▶ This coin celebrates the resettlement of Greeks from Egypt in Nîmes. Nile crocodiles were "hunted" in amphitheaters.

▼ The amphitheater of Nîmes was built to hold a huge crowd of spectators—as many as 25,000.

THE PEOPLE WHO LIVED IN THE northeastern part of Gaul were called the Treveri. During his visit to the provinces of Gaul, the emperor Augustus created a new city at Trier in 15–13 B.C.E. and named it Augusta Treverorum ("the city of the Treveri people founded by Augustus"). Much later the emperor Constantine lived here and built a cathedral, the biggest baths outside Rome itself, a palace, and a great basilica. Trier became a major imperial residence. The city declined in the fifth century C.E. after repeated attacks by barbarians.

▲ This wall painting from Trier may possibly be a portrait of Fausta, the wife of Constantine.

◀ The north gate in Trier's city wall, built in the late second century C.E., the Porta Nigra, or "Black Gate."

▼ Workers outside a country house—a fresco painting from Trier.

63

Buildings and Technology

"City of Rome District III called Isis and Serapis contains . . . a coin mint; the Colosseum amphitheater which has 45,000 seats; great training school for gladiators; house of Bruttius Prasesens; central theatrical storehouse; Shepherd's Fountain; Baths of Titus and Trajan; Portico of Livia; camp of the sailors of the Misenum fleet; 12 crossroads shrines; 2,757 blocks of apartments; 60 private houses; 18 storehouses; 80 baths; 16 bakeries."

THIS OFFICIAL CATALOG OF THE BUILDINGS in one of the 14 districts of Rome was made in the mid-fourth century C.E. It shows the huge number of buildings, especially blocks of apartments, in just one district of the city. The catalog ends with a summary of the most important buildings and structures in Rome. It includes 28 libraries, eight bridges, 11 forums, 10 basilicas, 11 public baths, 19 aqueducts, and 29 roads.

The Romans could build all this because they were good engineers and architects. They understood how structures stood up and developed the technology to build them. They learned some techniques from other peoples, especially the Etruscans, and they admired the temples and colonnades of the Greeks.

Section through a road

▲ This aqueduct, called Pont du Gard, was built in the time of the emperor Augustus to carry water to the city of Nîmes in Gaul from a source 30 miles (50 km) away.

◀ To build their road network the Romans needed surveyors who understood the landscape and how to measure it. You can see a surveyor here sighting a straight line using an instrument called a *groma*. The Romans tried to make their roads as straight as they could. The road surface was raised above ground level by pounding down layers of stone or gravel or whatever local materials were to hand.

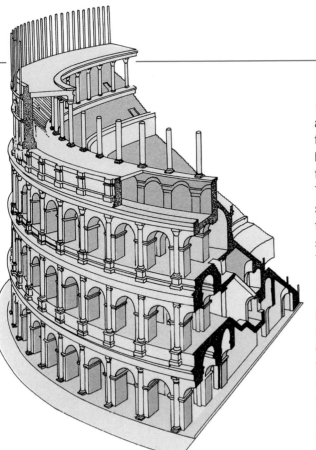

◀ This cross section through an amphitheater shows how the Romans were able to build tall structures that had to carry enormous weight. The circular series of arches spread out the load, including the weight of 45,000 spectators in the Colosseum.

▼ Just part of the water-powered mills at Barbegal near Arles in Gaul. Eight pairs of large wooden wheels, through a series of gears, drove the millstones. The water came from an aqueduct on top of a hill, and the excess water flowed into a great lake below.

The population of Arles is estimated to have been 80,000 in the early fourth century C.E. This great mill must have provided enough flour for all those people. It is still possible to see the remains of the mill building, the water channels, and the aqueduct.

Roads and communications

The Romans had better routes of communication than any previous people in the Mediterranean. The empire's road system began at the Great Forum in Rome and was marked by a golden milestone. In the provinces the first roads were built by the army to conquer new lands. A courier on imperial business, traveling by horse, changed horses regularly at official posting stations and could cover more than 144 miles (230 km) in 24 hours.

Water supply in the towns

The Romans needed a very large supply of water, not just for drinking but to fill their public baths and use in their lavatories. They brought water to towns in aqueducts (the word means "bringer of water"). In some places these were simple ditches, lined with wood or stone. But many towns had more elaborately built stone aqueducts that could carry water over long distances.

Inside the towns water was collected in basins and tanks and then distributed by underground pipes. A superintendent of the water supply in Rome named Frontinus wrote a manual in about 97 C.E. describing his work. He estimated that his aqueducts were able to supply Rome with 260 million gallons (1,200 l) of water every 24 hours.

Mills and other machinery

Although the Romans probably did not use wind power for mills, they did use water power. In many parts of the empire they built aqueducts to bring the right water pressure to power wheels, which drove grindstones to turn corn into flour. Smaller millstones were turned by animals or by slaves in the town bakeries.

The Romans invented a number of machines to carry out difficult tasks. The *vallus*, or reaping machine, was pushed by a horse against standing corn. A lifting device with a large wheel was used to take large blocks of stone up to tall structures, and complex machinery was built in amphitheaters for raising wild animals in their cages and releasing them in the arena. Water clocks were used to time speeches in the law courts. A boat powered by oxen turning paddle wheels was invented in the fourth century C.E. but was never built.

Roman machinery was made of wood and not metal. So it could not withstand constant stress. The gears in the Barbegal watermills (opposite) must have often needed repair.

Britain

"The population is very large, and there are very many farmhouses similar to those the Gauls build. There are a large number of cattle. For coins, they use bronze or gold or iron bars. Tin is found inland, and small quantities of iron near the coast. There is also timber of every kind. All the Britons . . . wear their hair long, and the men have mustaches."

THIS IS PART OF THE DESCRIPTION OF Britain by Julius Caesar in his book entitled *The War in Gaul.* The Romans were interested in conquering Britain for various reasons. Julius Caesar knew that his newly conquered province of Gaul would not be safe if Celtic troublemakers could escape to, and plan campaigns from, Britain.

The Romans also wanted to make sure that any new province could not only pay for itself but provide wealth for the central treasury. Caesar wrote about Britain's wealth of metals, and the geographer Strabo saw other possibilities for exports: leather, hunting dogs, and a supply of slaves. The province also supplied corn to the Rhine armies.

A series of invasions

Julius Caesar invaded Britain twice. The first time was in 55 B.C.E. and the second in 54 B.C.E. He did not leave any troops there. A century later the emperor Claudius decided to take an interest in what one Roman poet called "faraway Britain." Claudius wanted to win glory for himself by successfully completing a major military campaign. He knew that winning a war abroad would make him popular at home in Rome.

In 43 C.E. Claudius came to Britain to join his invasion army of about 40,000 soldiers after they had fought their way to the Thames River, causing much bloodshed. Claudius then led a great procession, including elephants for show, to take possession of the capital Camulodunum (now Colchester) in southeast England.

"Romanization" and prosperity

The emperor Claudius stayed only 16 days in Britain. The army's commander, Aulus Plautius, stayed on as the province's first governor. His army pushed on, toward the southwest at first, and began to conquer this new territory.

Building roads and forts as they went, the Romans steadily took control of most of England and Wales. But they never managed to conquer the whole island and they were forced to build a solid defensive wall

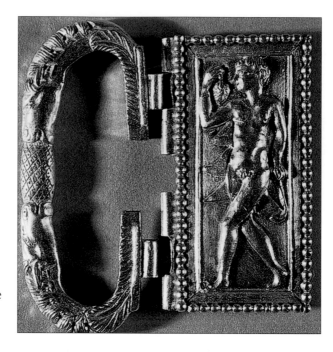

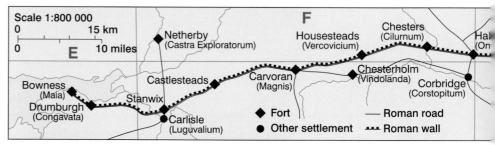

◄ In times of trouble people buried their wealth. This fine gold belt buckle, made in the late fourth century C.E., was part of the "Thetford hoard" found beside a Roman road in Norfolk, in eastern England.

▼ The Roman army built two permanent northern frontiers. The emperor Hadrian established the stone wall that bears his name, with its series of forts. Not many years later, the emperor Antoninus built a turf wall farther north.

◄ Building inscription from the fort of High Rochester, north of Hadrian's Wall. It records work done by men of the 20th Legion, sent from their base at Chester. The figures represent Mars (the god of war) and Hercules with his club.

in the far north—Hadrian's Wall—stretching for 73 miles (117 km) from west to east. Strong military garrisons were maintained in the north and west.

Apart from parts of mountainous Wales and northern Scotland, the rest of this remote island became "romanized." The road network grew. Towns developed where Roman army forts had been, or on the sites of British tribal settlements. Army veterans and their families established colonies. Romans and Britons intermarried, and farmers and villa owners grew rich in the countryside.

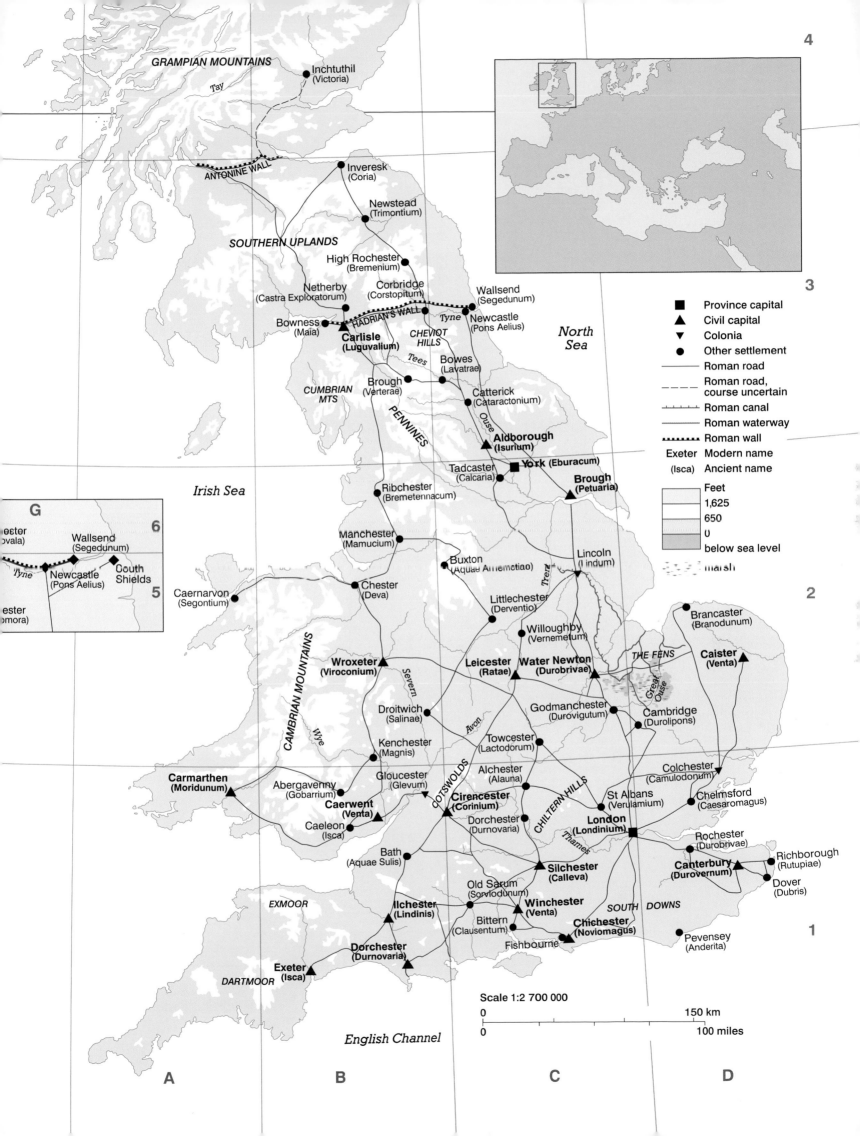

GRAMPIAN MOUNTAINS

Inchtuthil
(Victoria)

Tay

ANTONINE WALL

Inveresk
(Coria)

Newstead
(Trimontium)

SOUTHERN UPLANDS

High Rochester
(Bremenium)

Netherby
(Castra Exploratorum)

Corbridge
(Corstopitum)

Wallsend
(Segedunum)

Bowness
(Maia)

HADRIAN'S WALL

*CHEVIOT
HILLS*

Newcastle
(Pons Aelius)

Carlisle
(Luguvalium)

Tyne

Tees

Bowes
(Lavatrae)

North
Sea

*CUMBRIAN
MTS*

Brough
(Verterae)

Catterick
(Cataractonium)

PENNINES

Ouse

Aldborough
(Isurium)

Tadcaster
(Calcaria)

York (Eburacum)

Brough
(Petuaria)

Irish Sea

Ribchester
(Bremetennacum)

Manchester
(Mamucium)

Buxton
(Aquae Arnemetiae)

Lincoln
(Lindum)

Trent

Chester
(Deva)

Littlechester
(Derventio)

Caernarvon
(Segontium)

Willoughby
(Vernemetum)

Brancaster
(Branodunum)

THE FENS

Great Ouse

Caister
(Venta)

CAMBRIAN MOUNTAINS

Wroxeter
(Viroconium)

Leicester
(Ratae)

Water Newton
(Durobrivae)

Droitwich
(Salinae)

Severn

Godmanchester
(Durovigutum)

Cambridge
(Durolipons)

Avon

Kenchester
(Magnis)

Wye

Towcester
(Lactodorum)

Carmarthen
(Moridunum)

Abergavenny
(Gobarrium)

Gloucester
(Glevum)

COTSWOLDS

Alchester
(Alauna)

Colchester
(Camulodonum)

Cirencester
(Corinium)

CHILTERN HILLS

St Albans
(Verulamium)

Chelmsford
(Caesaromagus)

Caerwent
(Venta)

Caeleon
(Isca)

Dorchester
(Durnovaria)

London
(Londinium)

Rochester
(Durobrivae)

Bath
(Aquae Sulis)

Silchester
(Calleva)

Richborough
(Rutupiae)

Canterbury
(Durovernum)

EXMOOR

Ilchester
(Lindinis)

Old Sarum
(Sorviodunum)

Winchester
(Venta)

SOUTH DOWNS

Dover
(Dubris)

Bittern
(Clausentum)

Chichester
(Noviomagus)

Dorchester
(Durnovaria)

Fishbourne

Pevensey
(Anderita)

Exeter
(Isca)

DARTMOOR

English Channel

	Symbol legend
■	Province capital
▲	Civil capital
▼	Colonia
●	Other settlement
——	Roman road
- - -	Roman road, course uncertain
++++	Roman canal
——	Roman waterway
····	Roman wall
Exeter	Modern name
(Isca)	Ancient name

Feet
1,625
650
0
below sea level

marsh

Scale 1:2 700 000

0   150 km

0   100 miles

G

...ester
...ovala)

Wallsend
(Segedunum)

Tyne

Newcastle
(Pons Aelius)

South
Shields

...ester
...mora)

A   B   C   D

4

3

2

1

6

5

Hadrian's Wall, looking east near the fort at Housesteads.

Britain • Sites

Silchester

TOWNS IN THE ROMAN PROVINCE OF Britain developed in different ways. Some were established where a legion had once been stationed. Others were set up as colonies for retired soldiers. The Romans also encouraged settlements of the native tribes to develop into romanized towns.

In Hampshire the settlement of the Atrebates tribe was sited at a place known to the Romans as Calleva Atrebatum ("the town in the woods of the Atrebates"). Calleva, modern Silchester, became the capital of the region under Roman rule.

Calleva stood at a major crossroads in southern Britain. Near the road to Venta (Winchester) was a lodging house. Such buildings were situated on main roads throughout the province. Calleva was laid out in the usual Roman way, with straight streets crossing at right angles. Around 200 C.E. a new town wall was built of stone.

The town had the usual public buildings needed to establish a Roman way of life among people who had not experienced it before. The forum was right at the center where the main streets crossed. On one side of it was the basilica for the law courts, meetings, and ceremonies. Calleva had no theater, but there was an amphitheater outside the walls, as well as public baths and several temples. About 3,000 people probably lived in the town.

Wroxeter

WROXETER, IN THE WEST MIDLANDS of the province of Britain, has a very long history. In the first century C.E. it was the site for temporary forts as the army gradually pushed west in their occupation of the island. It then became a permanent legionary fortress. By the end of the first century the army had left and the site—with the streets of the fort intact—became a town for the local people.

The emperor Hadrian visited the province, and probably Wroxeter itself, in 122 C.E., and it was at this time that the building of new public facilities in the city were hurried toward completion. The city center had, in the mid-second century C.E., a large forum, an enclosed meat market, and public baths complete with lavatories. It had become the fourth largest town in Roman Britain and probably had a population of 5,000 people at its height.

At the end of Rome's control of its outer provinces, Wroxeter, unlike most other places, was redeveloped. Recent excavations have shown that the city center was rebuilt, in wood and in Roman architectural styles, around 542 C.E. But a century later, the Roman town was abandoned.

▼ Part of the excavated remains of Wroxeter. This wall (the highest to survive in Britain) is part of the cold room of the public baths, built of the local sandstone and lines of Roman tile. The large entrance once had double wooden doors through which the bathers entered the baths from the huge exercise hall.

◄ This aerial view of Silchester shows how archaeologists have been able to locate the streets of the town. Their hard stony surfaces have turned the crops in the fields a different color.

Palace at Fishbourne

THE MAGNIFICENT ROMAN PALACE AT Fishbourne in Sussex, in the south of England, must have been very costly to build. Who could have afforded to build it?

The king of the pre-Roman tribe called the Regni had been friendly toward Rome and helped the emperor Claudius in his invasion of Britain. This king, named Cogidubnus, was rewarded by the Romans for his support. He was allowed to remain king of the area and became a Roman citizen, probably ruling from the town of Noviomagus (Chichester). Claudius's invasion force may have landed at Fishbourne in 43 C.E. It is a suitable landing place, and the Roman army could rely on the support of Cogidubnus.

Archaeologists think that a large villa-style building was put up at Fishbourne a few years after Claudius's invasion. In about 75 C.E. it was most likely Cogidubnus who had the site landscaped and

◀ This second-century C.E. mosaic floor was probably laid by several mosaic craftsmen in charge of a number of workers. The center picture shows Cupid riding a dolphin. Seahorses, great jars, and scallop shells fill the other panels.

▲ Archaeologists have excavated nearly all the palace at Fishbourne. This model shows how impressive it was. The owner—thought to be Cogidubnus (who had romanized his name)— wanted to show that he really could live like a Roman.

a huge palace and gardens built. People coming to the palace by road from Chichester, or by boat, would have passed through a grand hallway and entered an enclosed, formally laid-out garden. The palace was built around the garden. It had private wings and a bath block.

Many of the rooms were heated with underfloor heating (the "hypocaust") and were finely decorated with wall paintings and mosaics. Craftsmen such as masons and carpenters probably came from Rome to work on the palace, but we also know from an inscription that there was a craft association in Chichester. There must have been plenty of work on the new Roman-style buildings. A new hypocaust was built only a few years before the palace burned to the ground in the late third century C.E.

The Roman Villa

"WHENEVER I'M WORN OUT WITH worry and want to get some rest, I go to my villa," wrote the poet Martial who was born in Bilbilis, Spain.

The Romans used the word *villa* to describe a variety of types of property, such as a simple farm, a large country estate employing hundreds of workers, a house in the country, or a seaside holiday home. Many rich Romans had farming estates scattered through the empire that brought them wealth from corn, vines, or olives. They might also have houses in the mountains or by the seaside.

Working farms

We know about Roman farms from some that have been excavated by archaeologists. The villa at Settefinestre between present-day Capalbio and Orbetello in central Italy (opposite) is one that has been carefully examined. We also know about farms from Roman writers such as Columella. In his book *About Farming* he wrote:

"A farm should be in a place with a healthy climate, with fertile soil, with some flat ground and some hilly, on an eastern or southern slope—but not too steep. The villa should have three sections: the 'villa urbana,' the house of the owner; the 'villa rustica,' the house of the farm manager and laborers; and the 'villa fructuaria,' the storehouses."

Country houses

Whether the owner's house was part of a large farm building as at Settefinestre or a country or seaside home, a Roman expected to enjoy all the amenities of a town house. The *atrium*, or enclosed courtyard, had various rooms around it—some were bedrooms, and one would be the *tablinum*, or main living room. There might be several *triclinia*, or dining rooms, positioned around the house to catch the afternoon sun throughout the year.

In town a family would visit the public baths. In their house in the country they would have their own set of bathrooms inside the house or in a separate block outside.

Villas of the north

The Roman villa was more important to the economy in the northern empire—Britain and Gaul—than in the Mediterranean region. The heavy soil of the north was suitable for the large-scale agriculture that could make villa farmers rich.

▲ We could easily use the modern word "villa" for this luxury seaside home from a wall painting at Pompeii. A number of these villas looked out over the Bay of Naples.

▶ The main building of this estate is on a slope, with formal gardens laid out in front. The living areas are built on top of the hill and the cellars (through the arches). Behind the colonnades on the front of the first floor were the family rooms, the baths, as well as wine and oil presses. The manager and slaves lived at the back of the house.

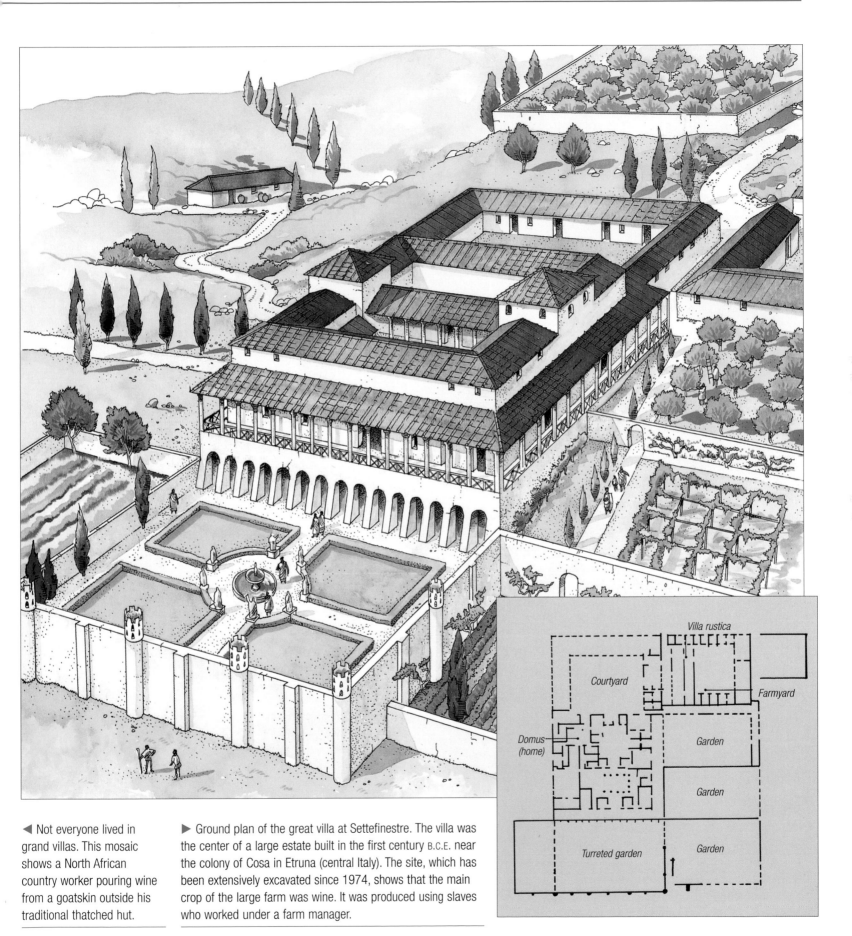

◀ Not everyone lived in grand villas. This mosaic shows a North African country worker pouring wine from a goatskin outside his traditional thatched hut.

▶ Ground plan of the great villa at Settefinestre. The villa was the center of a large estate built in the first century B.C.E. near the colony of Cosa in Etruna (central Italy). The site, which has been extensively excavated since 1974, shows that the main crop of the large farm was wine. It was produced using slaves who worked under a farm manager.

Villa rustica

Courtyard

Farmyard

Domus (home)

Garden

Garden

Turreted garden

Garden

The Danube

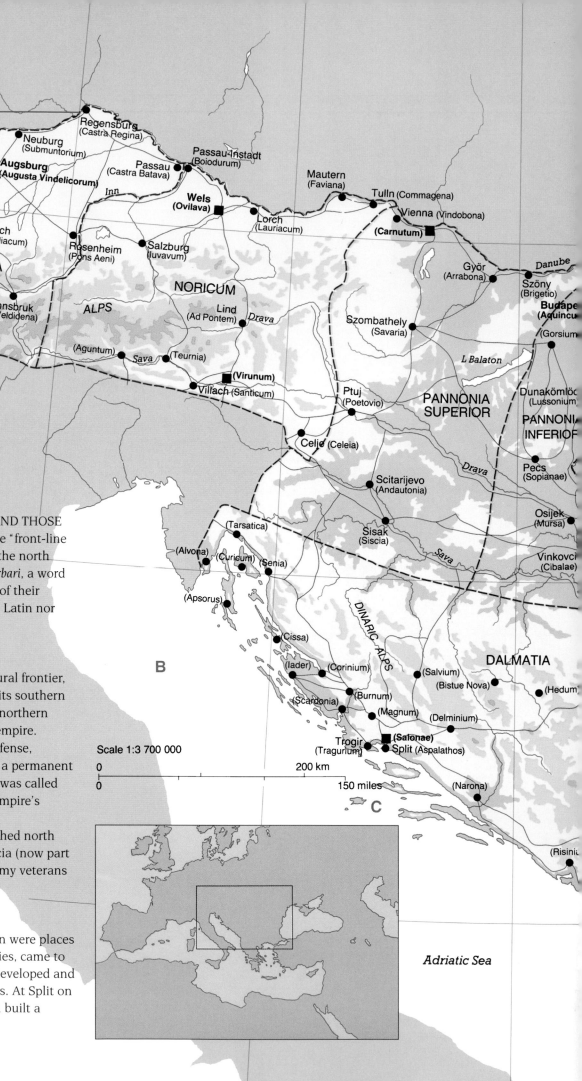

THE PROVINCES OF GERMANY AND THOSE just south of the Danube were the "front-line states" of the Roman Empire. To the north were the peoples the Romans called *barbari*, a word that they thought mimicked the sound of their speech. These barbarians neither spoke Latin nor lived like the Romans.

Natural frontier

The Danube River provided a good natural frontier, but many legionary forts were built on its southern banks. Soldiers were recruited in these northern provinces to fight in other parts of the empire.

At the weak point in the northern defense, between the Rhine and Danube Rivers, a permanent barrier with a patrol road was built—it was called the limes. The Black Sea provided the empire's northeastern boundary.

By 106 C.E. the Roman army had pushed north and conquered the new province of Dacia (now part of Romania). Towns and colonies for army veterans and their families were built there.

Growth of towns

The legionary forts of the Danube region were places where traders, as well as soldiers' families, came to live. Small villages, known as *canabae*, developed and eventually became proper Roman towns. At Split on the Adriatic Sea the emperor Diocletian built a seaside palace for his retirement.

2

Legend

- ■ Province capital
- ● Other settlement
- – – – Province boundary
- —— Roman road
- Istanbul Modern name
- (Byzantium) Ancient name

Feet
6,500
3,250
650
0

▶ The earth and stone amphitheater at Carnuntum could hold 13,000 spectators. To the left you can see traces in the ground left by Roman houses and shops.

Casei (Samum)
Moigrad (Porolissum)
Cluj (Napoca)
Alba Iulia (Apulum)
(Angustia)
Tisza
Muresul
Oltul
(Cumidava)
(Ulpia Traiana Sarmizegetusa)
(Sarmizegetusa)
DACIA
(Praetorium)
(Castra Traiana)
(Troesmis)
Sarduc (Centum Putei)
TRANSYLVANIAN ALPS
(Ulmetum)
Mitrovica (Sirmium)
Palanka (Lederata)
Mehadia (Ad Mediam)
Turnu-Severin (Drobeta)
(Pons Aluti)
Belgrade (Singidunum)
Kostolac (Viminacium)
(Heracleia)
(Aureus Mons)
Kaliste (Municipium)
Brza Palanka (Egeta)
Adamclisi (Tropaeum Traiani)
MOESIA SUPERIOR
(Durostorum)
Mangalia (Callatis)
(Maluesa)
Cuprija (Horreum Margi)
Danube
Celei (Sucidava)
Archar (Ratiaria)
Morava
(Montana)
(Oescus)
(Novae)
(Marcianopolis)
Varna (Odessus)
Nis (Naissus)
Nisava
MOESIA INFERIOR
Lovech (Melta)
Nicopolis ad Istrum
Black Sea
Sofia (Serdica)
BALKAN MOUNTAINS
Nesebur (Mesembria)
Ulpianum
Stara Zagora (Beroe)
(Deultum)
Drin
Maritsa
Philippopolis (Plovdiv)
Skopje (Scupi)
RHODOPE MOUNTAINS
(Scodra)
THRACIA
Edirne (Hadrianopolis)
Vize (Bizye)
(Lissus)
Istanbul (Byzantium)
Nicopolis ad Nestum
Komotini (Porsule)
(Perinthus)
Apri (Theodosiopolis)
Sea of Marmara
(Doriscus)
(Aphrodisias)
Aegean Sea

D   E   F   G

Greece and the Southern Balkans

Greek language and culture

The Romans admired Greek civilization, as this quotation shows:

"I prefer that a boy should learn Greek as his first language. He will soon pick up Latin, whether he likes it or not, as it is in general use. At the same time, he ought first to be instructed in Greek learning, from which ours is derived."—Quintilian.

The author of the quotation, Quintilian, became the first Roman "university professor" in Athens. He was also tutor to the emperor Vespasian's children. Rich Romans sent their sons (but not their daughters) to Athens to complete their education.

Three provinces of Greece

The Romans divided the Southern Balkans into three provinces, with a governor in charge of each. Achaea in the south was still the center of the old Greek civilization. Under the Romans several of its cities and sacred places such as Delphi were restored and rebuilt.

Much of this restoration and building went on in the second century C.E. A wealthy Athenian named Herodes Atticus was responsible for a variety of

▲ This delicate carving in marble shows Christ as the Greek god Apollo playing the lyre.

▼ Part of the Via Egnatia, the Roman military highway that linked the Adriatic port of Dyrrachiumm with Thessalonica and points east.

public buildings, including a theater in Athens, an aqueduct at Olympia, a stadium at Delphi, and healing pools for the sick at Thermopylae.

In the north, Thessalonica became the provincial capital of Macedonia. It was an important port on the route to the eastern empire and was connected to the Adriatic Sea by the Via Egnatia. Thessalonica became a Roman colony in the middle of the third century and it was an occasional imperial residence. It was enlarged in the fifth century, when massive town walls, the church St. Demetrius, and a new palace for use of the prefect were built.

Early Christianity

Greece under the Romans is also associated with Christianity. It was to Greece that St. Paul came on his second journey. He was arrested at the Roman colony of Philippi after a riot and was released only when he was discovered to be a Roman citizen. Paul later preached in Athens and Corinth.

▼ About half of the 5-mile- (8-km-) long walls of Thessalonica, built in the fifth century, survives.

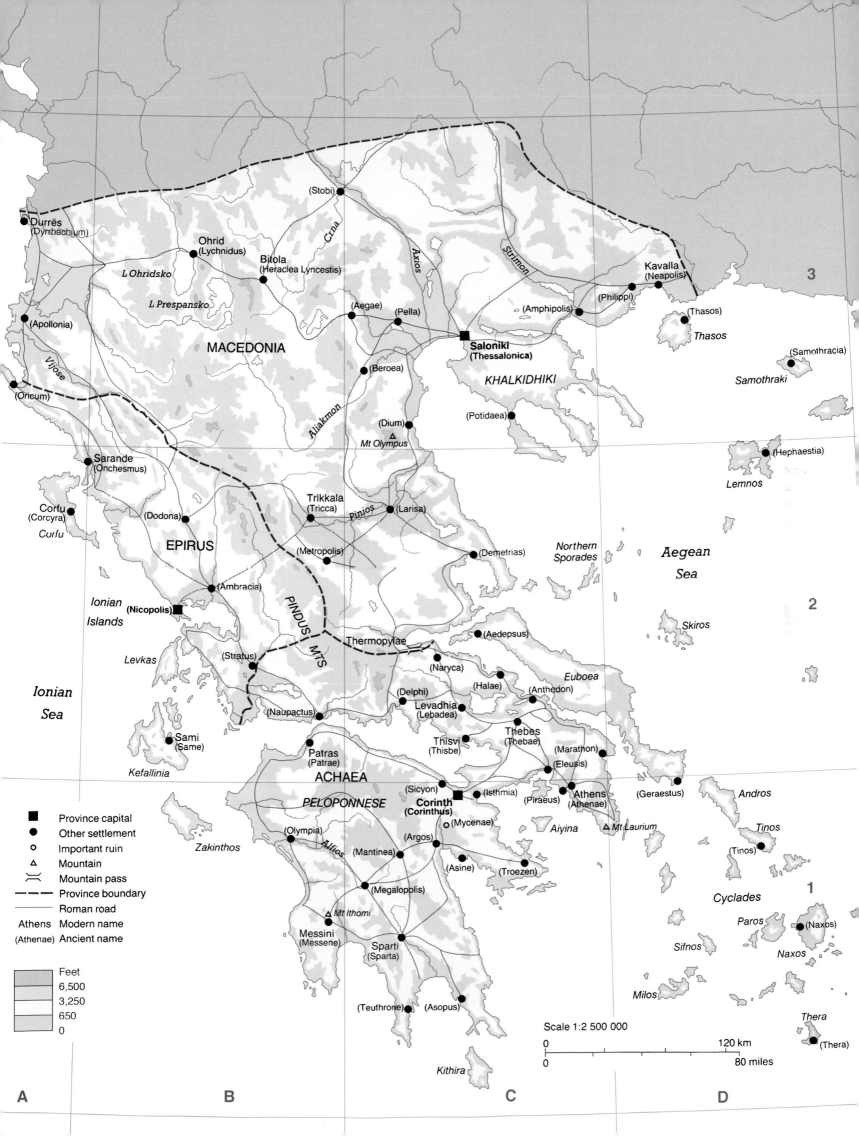

Durrës
(Dyrrhachium)

Ohrid
(Lychnidus)

Bitola
(Heraclea Lyncestis)

L Ohridsko

L Prespansko

(Apollonia)

Vijose

(Oricum)

(Stobi)

Crna

Axios

Strimon

(Aegae)

(Pella)

MACEDONIA

(Beroea)

(Amphipolis)

Kavalla
(Neapolis)

(Philippi)

(Thasos)

Thasos

**Saloniki
(Thessalonica)**

KHALKIDHIKI

(Samothracia)

Samothraki

Sarande
(Onchesmus)

(Dium)

△
Mt Olympus

(Potidaea)

(Hephaestia)

Lemnos

Aliakmon

Corfu
(Corcyra)

Corfu

(Dodona)

Trikkala
(Tricca)

Pinios

(Larisa)

EPIRUS

(Metropolis)

(Demetrias)

*Northern
Sporades*

*Aegean
Sea*

Skiros

(Ambracia)

(Nicopolis)

*Ionian
Islands*

PINDUS

MTS

Thermopylae

(Aedepsus)

Euboea

(Naryca)

(Anthedon)

(Halae)

Levkas

(Stratus)

(Naupactus)

(Delphi)

Levadhia
(Lebadea)

Thebes
(Thebae)

(Marathon)

*Ionian
Sea*

Sami
(Same)

Patras
(Patrae)

Kefallinia

ACHAEA

Thisvi
(Thisbe)

(Eleusis)

(Isthmia)

(Piraeus)

Athens
(Athenae)

(Geraestus)

Andros

Tinos

PELOPONNESE

(Sicyon)

**Corinth
(Corinthus)**

(Mycenae)

Aiyina

△ *Mt Laurium*

(Tinos)

(Olympia)

Alfios

(Mantinea)

(Argos)

(Asine)

(Troezen)

Zakinthos

Cyclades

(Megalopolis)

△*Mt Ithomi*

Paros

(Naxos)

Messini
(Messene)

Sparti
(Sparta)

Sifnos

Naxos

Milos

(Teuthrone)

(Asopus)

Thera

(Thera)

Kithira

■ Province capital
● Other settlement
○ Important ruin
△ Mountain
)(Mountain pass
--- Province boundary
― Roman road
Athens Modern name
(Athenae) Ancient name

Feet
6,500
3,250
650
0

Scale 1:2 500 000

0   120 km

0   80 miles

A   B   C   D

3

2

1

Athens—city of splendor

MUCH OF ANCIENT ATHENS WAS destroyed by the armies of the consul Sulla in the first century B.C.E. Several Roman emperors later rebuilt and added to the city, recreating the glory of this center of classical Greek civilization. Both Julius Caesar and the emperor Augustus put up public buildings. The emperor Hadrian carried out many public works. The millionaire Herodes Atticus built an odeum, or concert theater, that held more than 5,000 people.

The emperor Hadrian in Athens

Hadrian first visited Athens in 124–25 C.E. and by the end of his reign in 138 C.E. he had almost transformed the city. He completed a huge temple to the Greek god Zeus (called Jupiter by the Romans), which had been started long before in the sixth century B.C.E. He built a temple dedicated to all the Greeks. During his three winters in Athens, Hadrian also saw work finished on an aqueduct, a gymnasium, a huge library, and a bridge.

Hadrian also erected a triumphal arch on an ancient street that led from the old city of Athens to the new Roman section that he had built. The arch carries two inscriptions. On one side it reads, "This is Athens, the ancient city of Theseus," but on the other it proclaims, "This is the city of Hadrian and not of Theseus."

▶ Inside this first-century B.C.E. "Tower of the Winds" was a 24-hour clock driven by water power. It is decorated with wall sculptures showing the "eight winds."

▼ A bronze bust of the emperor Hadrian, who loved ancient Greece and rebuilt Athens. His decorated breastplate shows soldiers fighting.

▲ The Acropolis of Athens, with the Parthenon, the Greek temple of the city's goddess. On the slope below is the odeum of Herodes Atticus.

Corinth—destroyed then rebuilt

CORINTH WAS A WEALTHY AND IMPORTANT city in the Greek world. One Roman writer described it as "that beautiful city full of treasures of every kind."

In the middle of the second century B.C.E. Corinth tried to fight against the Romans along with other cities in Achaea. The result was terrible for Corinth. The Roman consul Lucius Mummius was sent to Greece with a large fleet and an army. He completely destroyed Corinth (setting it on fire), made all of its people slaves, and carried off all its art treasures.

More than 100 years later Julius Caesar chose the site of Corinth to establish a colony for retired soldiers from Italy. He set about reconstructing some of the ruined buildings and planning a new city, complete with an impressive city center. Roman Corinth became a major trading and business center and it quickly recovered its commercial prosperity. It also became the seat of government for the Roman southern province of Achaea.

Restoring the Greek city

Standing above every other building in Corinth was the temple to the Greek god Apollo. Built in the sixth century B.C.E., it was restored by the Romans. The approach to the city center was along a wide road (later called the Lechaeum Road) that ran more than a third of a mile from the harbor. Entry from that road into the forum or *agora* (as the Greeks called it) was by way of a grand triumphal arch. The forum was the town's main business area and was surrounded by a number of colonnaded buildings.

Some of the most important buildings here were the basilicas. These large halls were used for meetings and law courts. Corinth was the capital city of Greece in Roman times, so there was a lot of business and administration for the governor and officials to carry out. In 52 C.E. the apostle Paul preached here.

The second-century C.E. millionaire Herodes Atticus paid for an odeum to be built at Corinth, as well as the one in Athens. Cut into the rock, this small theater could seat an audience of 3,000. Herodes Atticus also rebuilt an elaborate public fountain in the center of the city.

Corinth was destroyed a second time by an earthquake in 521 C.E.

▲ Stone seats at the theater at Corinth. Built originally by the Greeks, it was remodeled by the Romans.

▼ Plan of Roman Corinth. The Romans added a number of temples to the city center.

The Corinth canal

One of the sights of modern Greece is the canal that joins the Gulf of Corinth to the Aegean Sea. Julius Caesar wanted to build a canal but it was the early emperors who carried out the project. The emperor Caligula surveyed the ground and the emperor Nero actually started digging in 67 C.E.—or rather his 6,000 Jewish war-slaves did. The modern canal was completed in 1893.

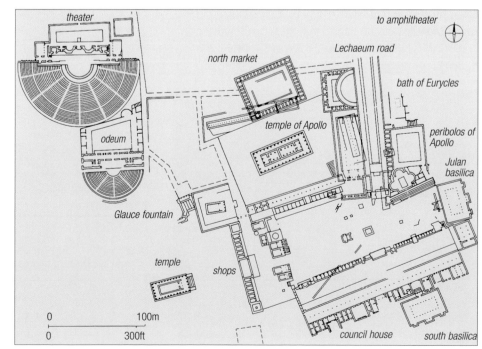

Asia Minor

THE ROMANS FIRST BECAME INTERESTED in Asia Minor during the reign of the Seleucid king Antiochus III. He was defeated by the Romans in two land battles and one at sea in 190 B.C.E. Three other kings gave their territories to the Romans. This left only Lycia and Cilicia for the Romans to conquer.

Pirates

These areas were well known for being the haunt of pirates who lived on land but hunted down ships traveling in this part of the Mediterranean. After many campaigns against them they were crushed by Pompey the Great in 67 B.C.E.

There were a number of important Greek cities already established before the Roman occupation, especially along the coast. The emperor Augustus set up most of the Roman colonies in Asia Minor—for example, at Antiochia, Olbasa, and Iconium. Augustus built a special road to link these new colonies. Elsewhere the Romans used and improved on the road system that already existed.

Roman Cyprus

Until Cyprus was made Roman in 58 B.C.E. it had been part of Egyptian territory for nearly 250 years. The capital of the island was Paphus, but the port of Salamis became the biggest city and the main center of trade.

The Romans exported much of the island's raw materials, including timber and copper (from the state mines) and corn. Those who exploited Cyprus became rich, but the island suffered as a result. Christianity was introduced to Cyprus following a visit by the apostle Paul in 45 C.E.

◀ This mosaic was made in the fourth century C.E. for a house in the town of Curium on the south coast of Cyprus. There is also a well-preserved theater nearby.

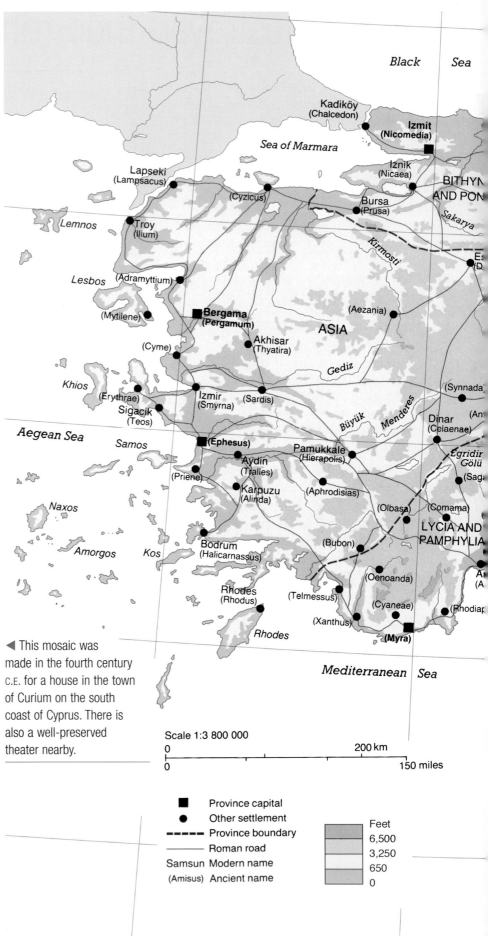

Scale 1:3 800 000

■	Province capital
●	Other settlement
-------	Province boundary
———	Roman road
Samsun	Modern name
(Amisus)	Ancient name

Feet
6,500
3,250
650
0

A   B

5

Sinop
(Sinope)

(Amastris)   Inebolu
                                  (Abonuteichus)   *Black Sea*

PONTINE   MOUNTAINS

Eregli   Samsun
(Heraclea Pontica)   (Amisus)   4

(Claudiopolis)   (Side)   (Trapezus)

                                              (Eupatoria)

           (Gangra)   (Amasea)   *Kelkit*
                                                                                           (Satala)
                                                         (Comana Pontica)   (Nicopolis)

Ankara   *Euphrates*
(Ancyra)   (Tavium)   Sivas
                                                          (Megalopolis)

(Pessinus)   3

                    Tuz   *Kızıl Irmak*   CAPPADOCIA
                    Gölü
GALATIA   **Kayseri**   Malatya
                                             (Mazaca)   (Melitene)

                              (Garsaura)
Beyşehir   (Cucusus)
Gölü   (Tyana)   2

Konya   (Anazarbus)
(Iconium)   (Podandus)

(Isaura)   Karaman   Ataniya
                      (Laranda)   (Adana)
CILICIA   **(Tarsus)**   (Issus)
TAURUS MOUNTAINS   (Soli)
Selimiye   (Claudiopolis)
(Side)
Gazipasa   Silifke   (Elaeusa)
(Selinus)   (Seleucia)

                                                    (Carpasia)

              Lapithos
Cyprus   (Lapethus)   1
                                      (Salamis)
(Limenia)   (Tamassus)
Paphus   Larnaca
                                    (Citium)
         (Curium)   (Amathus)

D   E   F

Ephesus—Asian capital

WHEN KING ATTALUS III GAVE HIS kingdom to the Romans in his will in 133 B.C.E., the city of Ephesus became the capital of the new province of Asia and the governor lived here. It had already been a wealthy city under the Greeks and was famous for its temple to the goddess Artemis, one of the Seven Wonders of the World in ancient times. Originally on the sea (the coastline has now moved), Ephesus was an important port.

During the Greek period a wall enclosed the city and connected it with the harbor and the coast. An impressive road lined with columns (rather like the

▶ It was along this paved road that the procession for the festival of Artemis (who was called Diana by the Romans) led from her temple to the theater.

◀ Impressive entrance to the temple of the emperor Hadrian, which was built in the early second century C.E. Emperors were often worshiped as gods, especially away from Rome.

▼ If you were rich enough you could own a grand town house like this in the city center. The walls of this room are painted to make it look as if they are covered with marble.

Lechaeum Road in Corinth) ran from the harbor to the theater. This theater was first built in the third century B.C.E. Roman rebuilding, begun in 41 C.E., took 80 years to complete. Afterwards, the theater held about 25,000 spectators.

The city was also famous for its library, which was built during the second century C.E. in honor of Celsus, one of the governors.

St. Paul in Ephesus

St. Paul, on his third journey, visited Ephesus and caused a riot there. His Christian teachings particularly upset the silversmiths who made offerings for those who worshiped the goddess Artemis. They feared that the introduction of Christianity would put them out of business.

A silversmith called Demetrius addressed a huge crowd in the city's theater, complaining about the disrespect to their goddess and lack of trade. The crowd shouted: "Great is Artemis, goddess of the people of Ephesus!" The town clerk had to calm the crowds and tell them that they could make official complaints to the governor. After this episode, Paul had to leave Ephesus for Greece.

Aphrodisias—theater, temple, and baths

THE NAME OF THIS CITY COMES FROM ITS patron goddess Aphrodite. She was the Greek goddess of love and beauty, called Venus by the Romans. Aphrodisias was a popular visiting place both with first-century B.C.E. generals such as Sulla and Julius Caesar and with the emperors Augustus and Hadrian.

Aphrodite's temple at Aphrodisias was built in the first century B.C.E. In the second century C.E. the emperor Hadrian had a special courtyard put up around it. In the sixth century, like many other Greek and Roman temples, Aphrodite's temple became a Christian church.

This was an important area for the supply of fine-quality marble. Marble from Aphrodisias was exported to many parts of the Roman world. It was also a city noted for its arts, especially stone carving. The influence of artists working at Aphrodisias spread as far as North Africa.

City entertainments

In the second century C.E. the great theater was converted so that it could be used as an amphitheater—for gladiator shows and wild-beast fights. There were also other buildings that were used for public entertainment.

Just in front of the temple of Aphrodite is the site of the odeum, where concerts and recitals took place. The city also had a stadium for athletics and chariot-racing. (Now under grass, the site is at the very top of the aerial photograph.) In about 265 C.E. most of the city was enclosed and protected by a great wall, which even went around the city's stadium. The people and the authorities of Aphrodisias were worried about invasions of the Goths.

Another favorite Roman pastime was going to the public baths. Hadrian built a very large bath block for the people of Aphrodisias. (Its remains are on the far left of the photograph.)

▶ This aerial view of Aphrodisias shows the theater built into the slope of the natural high point of the Greek town—the acropolis. At the top of the picture you can see the tall columns of Aphrodite's temple. At the bottom right are piles of stones from the excavations. There is still much to be discovered here by archaeologists.

Town and City Life

"There's no peace or quiet in the city for the poor. Early in the morning schoolmasters stop us from having any normal life. Before it gets light we have the bakers. Then it's hammering of the coppersmiths all day."

THIS IS HOW THE POET MARTIAL DESCRIBED living in Rome. Another writer, Juvenal, mentioned that there were narrow streets "jammed with carts and their swearing drivers, crowded with people pushing and shoving, pavements and roads filthy underfoot."

Roman towns and cities were certainly very crowded. Shops, craftspeople, and shouting traders would fill the streets.

How people shopped

Shops advertised their goods with painted signs (such as a leg of pork for a butcher) or a written notice. All towns had *thermopolia*—hot food for a quick snack on the premises or to take away. Many businesses were family-run, often with slave assistants and young apprentices.

Goods and food were not prepackaged. You bought your bread at the place where it was first ground into flour, then made into dough, and finally baked. If you wanted a pair of sandals, the cobbler would make them for you on the spot. Knives and other tools were made and sold by the ironmonger at his shop.

Housing conditions

Martial and Juvenal complained about the living conditions of the poor in towns. They lived mostly in run-down blocks of apartments, often above shops. In Rome these might be six stories high—although this was less common in other towns. Mostly built of wood, these apartments often burned to the ground.

People who were rich were able to get some quiet in town. In Rome they built their homes away from the bustling streets, up on the hillsides. Houses of the well-to-do were enclosed, with tucked-away private courtyards. They were cool in the summer and had their own kitchen, dining room, bedrooms, slave quarters, and back garden.

Streets

Under the streets went the sewage and water pipes. Water usually poured into stone basins or troughs at the edge of the road. Most people did not have a private water supply and so they collected their water from these troughs.

In many towns the roads, and sometimes the pavements, were paved with stone.

◀ A shopkeeper reaches up to a shelf. We see evidence of Roman daily life in sculpture, such as these memorials on the tombs of shopkeepers and craftspeople from various parts of the empire.

▲ A lady sits with a shopping list written on a wax tablet, waiting for the butcher to prepare her order. Note the weighing scales, the three-legged chopping block, and the hanging joints of meat.

▶ Street life in a Roman town. "We live in a city shored up with slender props—for that's how the landlords stop the houses from falling down. The place to live is where there are no fires."—Juvenal.

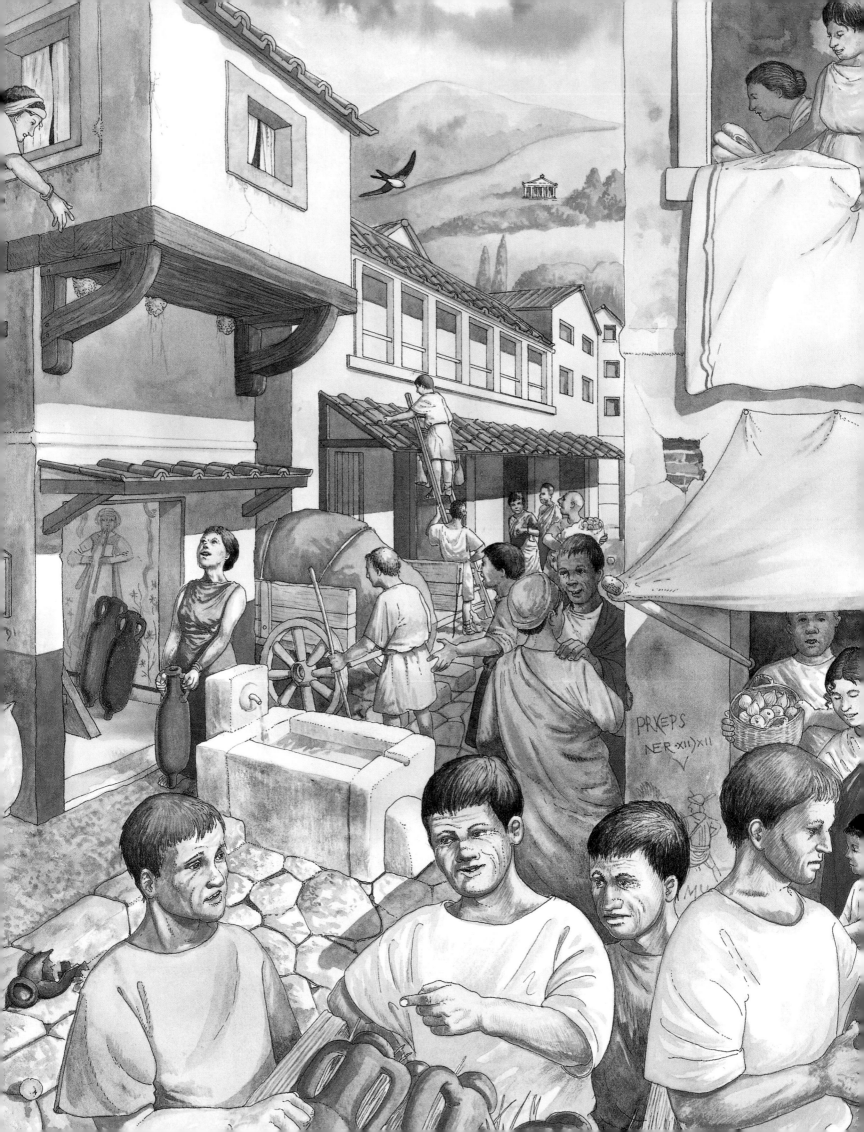

The Exotic East

THE AREA THAT BECAME THE EASTERN provinces of the Roman Empire was originally ruled by a number of kings. The Romans often made treaties with them and then took over the government of the area.

This happened first of all in Judaea in 6 C.E., although the Romans did not take full control of this area until 44 C.E. Even then the Jews of Judaea often rebelled against Roman rule. Syria became Roman in 64 C.E., Arabia in 106, and Mesopotamia in 114.

Keeping the Roman peace

The emperor Trajan established a frontier to the empire on the eastern edge of Arabia and Syria. A network of stone-paved roads was laid across the desert, and soldiers occupied strongly built forts. These forts were often square, with large round towers at each corner.

Trajan sent six legions to occupy this area and pacify the peoples. The presence of so many soldiers, their forts, and their roads helped establish trade between this area and Rome.

Trade with the east

Many goods were exported from the east to other parts of the Roman Empire—timber, cloth, glass, and leather goods, for example. The port of Tyrus in the eastern Mediterranean was well known for its purple dye, which the Romans used to color their clothes. The Romans also used a lot of sweet-smelling substances such as frankincense and myrrh in the preparation of incense, perfumes, and medicines.

Much of this trade was through Arabia, and the goods were carried by camel. A camel train could cover about 20 miles (32 km) in a day, according to Roman writers. The desert city of Palmyra became an important trading destination for camel trains. There was even trade across the desert with India (for spices) and with China (for silk). Along with this trade, many easterners came west to Rome.

Wild animals

Many provinces provided exotic animals for "sport" and slaughter in amphitheaters all over the empire, but especially for Rome itself. Trade in ivory and ebony from Africa also flourished.

The town of Hierapolis in northern Syria became the depot where animals were collected and shipped south—beasts such as tigers, lions, leopards, and wild asses. They probably traveled to the Egyptian port of Alexandria for shipment to Rome.

▶ The remains of the massive first-century C.E. temple to the chief god Jupiter at Heliopolis (now Baalbek) in the province of Syria.

▶ View from the citadel, or hilltop fortress, at Edessa in Mesopotamia.

▼ This mosaic from a tomb in Edessa shows a rich family. Although it is a Roman province, they wear their traditional clothes, and their names are written in the regional language, Syriac.

5

Samsat
(Samosata)

(Antinonopolis)

TUR ABDIN

Urfa
(Edessa)

Nusaybin
(Nisibis)

(Zeugma)

Harran
(Carrhae)

(Alexandria ad Issum)

(Cyrrhus)

Membij
(Hierapolis)

MESOPOTAMIA

(Singara)

Aleppo
(Beroea)

Antakya
(Antiochia)

Raqqa (Nic Horium)

Euphrates

(Laodicea)

Orontes

(Apamea)

SYRIA

Risafe
(Resapha)

Khabir

Buseire
(Circesium)

Mediterranean Sea

Hama
(Epiphania)

(Seriane)

4

(Raphanaea)

Homs
(Emesa)

(Palmyra)

(Dura-Europus)

Tripoli
(Tripolis)

(Danaba)

SYRIAN DESERT

Beirut
(Berytus)

Baalbek
(Heliopolis)

■ Province capital

● Other settlement

▬ ▬ Province boundary

Saida
(Sidon)

Roman road

Tyre
(Tyrus)

Damascus

Homs   Modern name

(Caesarea Paneas)

(Emesa)   Ancient name

3

Sea of
Galilee

El Qanawat
(Canatha)

Feet

6,500

Tiberias

3,250

Nazareth

650

(Lejjun)

Um Qeis
(Gadara)

0

(Caesarea Maritima)

Below sea level

(Scythopolis)

Busra
(Bostra)

Seasonal river

Tel Aviv-Yafo
(Joppa)

(Neapolis)

Jarash
(Gerasa)

JUDAEA

(Diospolis)

Jericho

Amman
(Philadelphia)

(Ascalon)

Bethlehem

Jerusalem (Aelia Capitolina)

Gaza

(Herodion)

Hebron

(Madaba)

▶ A mosaic from a villa near
Antiochia. It could be called
"Still Life with Boiled Eggs."
Mosaics can tell us about
everyday life long ago.

(Masada)

Dead
Sea

2

Beersheba
(Berosaba)

Karnak
(Characmoba)

ARABIA

(Oboda)

(Nessana)

NEGEV DESERT

(Petra)

Scale 1:3 500 000

0   120 km

0   100 miles

87

1

Elat
(Aila)

A   B   C   D

Oasis city of Palmyra

"The tax collector shall exact ... for a camel-load of dried foodstuffs ... for purple wool by the fleece ... for myrrh imported in goatskins ... for each donkey-load of olive oil"—customs regulations, Palmyra, 137 C.E.

PALMYRA WAS AN OASIS (A FERTILE SPOT) in the Syrian desert. It was an important site in Syrian-Babylonian trade by the first century B.C.E. It was also a caravan city. Camel and donkey trains bringing luxury goods from India, China, and Arabia passed through Palmyra on their way to coastal ports such as Tyrus and Sidon.

▼ The ruins of the oasis of Palmyra. Beyond the trees of the fertile area lies the desert. Caravans passed this way to and from the Euphrates River and the Persian Gulf.

Magnificent buildings

In the middle of the second century C.E. a whole series of public buildings was started. Most impressive was the wide street lined with columns that ran nearly half a mile (0.8 km) across the city.

The buildings on the edge of the city include an enormous temple to the god Bel, one of the most important gods worshiped in Babylonia to the east. There were other temples dedicated to the locally worshiped gods.

Other notable buildings included the Arch of Triumph. The city's forum must have served as a place for caravans to load and unload.

Masada

THE JEWISH PEOPLE WERE INVOLVED IN several rebellions against rule by foreigners. In 66 C.E. they rose up in arms against the Roman troops stationed in Jerusalem. Rome then sent an army of around 50,000 men to crush the rebellion. Jerusalem was recaptured in 70 C.E. Large numbers of people died.

The Romans may have thought the rebellion was over. But one Jewish group, called the Zealots, continued the fight. In 66 C.E. they had taken over the mountain fortress of Masada. We have a vivid account of the siege seven years later from the Jewish historian called Josephus.

Mountain siege

Josephus describes how the commander of the Roman army, Flavius Silva, built a great ramp against the mountain so his army could break in: "On top of this ramp they constructed a pier of stones and on that built a tower 90 ft [27m] high protected all over with plates of iron."

Despite their fortified position, the Jews knew they could not hold out against the Romans: 960 Jews chose suicide rather than surrender. A woman and her five children who hid in a water cistern gave the account of Masada's last days to Josephus.

▼ Herodion, King Herod's fortified mountaintop palace, from the air. Notice the four round towers built in the perimeter walls.

► View of Masada with (on the left) the ramp built by the Romans. Traces of the square Roman army camps are visible.

Egypt

E GYPT WAS CONQUERED BY KING Alexander the Great of Macedonia in 330 B.C.E. Alexander founded the city of Alexandria, which grew into a great center of Greek culture and influence. After his death a Macedonian general called Ptolemy established himself as king. After him, all Egyptian kings were called Ptolemy.

Last of the Ptolemies

The Romans became interested in Egypt in the second century B.C.E., and gradually began to assert their authority there. By the first century B.C.E. a Ptolemy was only on the throne of Egypt because the Romans wanted him there.

When the Ptolemy who was nicknamed Auletes ("Flute player") died, his will named his daughter, Cleopatra, and his son, Ptolemy, to succeed him jointly. But he appointed Rome as their guardians. In 30 B.C.E. the emperor Augustus "added Egypt to the empire of the Roman people."

Corn for Rome

The capital and main port of Egypt—Alexandria— was the second largest city in the Roman Empire. From here the province exported huge quantities of corn. Rome needed these large supplies—more than 200,000 Romans registered for free corn in 2 B.C.E., for example.

With the annual flooding of the Nile River, Egypt was certainly fertile enough to provide this and all the corn it needed for its own population of about 7 million. Other exports from Egypt included papyrus (for writing on—the Romans did not have paper), flax for making cloth, as well as perfumes, medicines, olives, and dates.

Cyrenaica and Crete

Cyrenaica, a region 500 miles (800 km) to the west of Egypt along the North African coast, became a Roman province in 74 B.C.E. It had originally been an area of Greek colonies and was now governed together with Crete as a single province. The most important city was Cyrene. The city was badly damaged in 115 C.E. during the Jewish Revolt, but it was restored with the help of the emperor Hadrian.

Crete, home of the ancient Minoan civilization, was conquered by the Romans in 69–67 B.C.E. The Roman general Quintus Metellus, and three legions, brutally occupied the island. It was prosperous during the Roman period, and there were many country villas on the island.

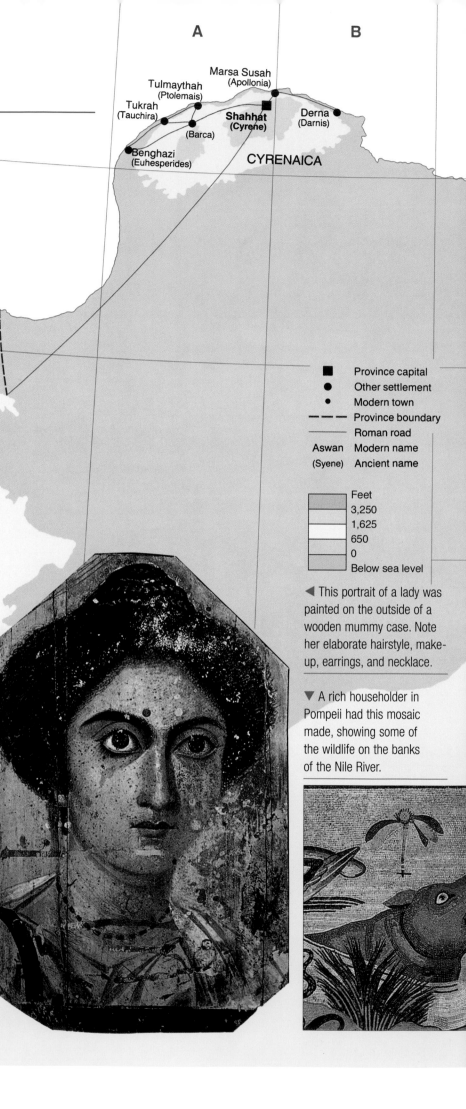

A **B**

Marsa Susah (Apollonia)
Tulmaythah (Ptolemais)
Tukrah (Tauchira)
Shahhat (Cyrene)
Derna (Darnis)
(Barca)
Benghazi (Euhesperides)
CYRENAICA

■ Province capital
● Other settlement
• Modern town
--- Province boundary
— Roman road
Aswan Modern name
(Syene) Ancient name

Feet
3,250
1,625
650
0
Below sea level

◀ This portrait of a lady was painted on the outside of a wooden mummy case. Note her elaborate hairstyle, make-up, earrings, and necklace.

▼ A rich householder in Pompeii had this mosaic made, showing some of the wildlife on the banks of the Nile River.

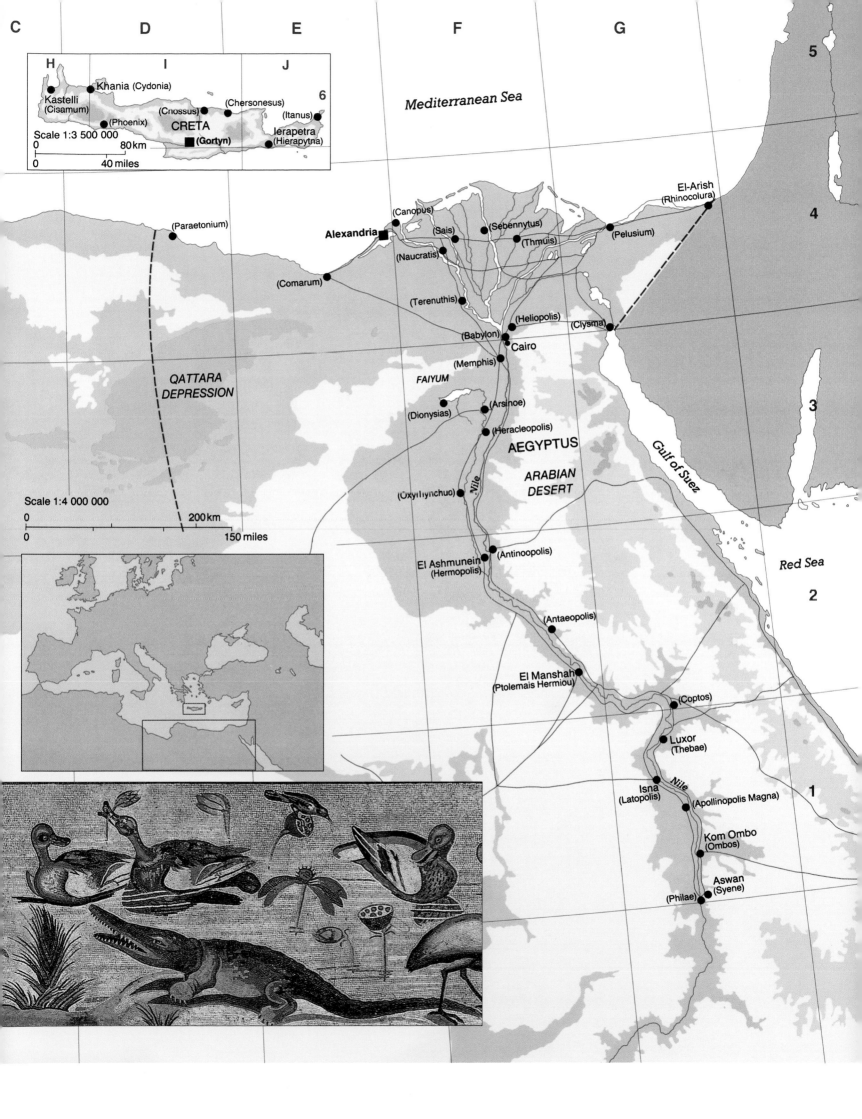

C   D   E   F   G

5

CRETA inset:

H   I   J

6

Kastelli (Cisamum)

Khania (Cydonia)

(Phoenix)

(Cnossus)

(Chersonesus)

(Itanus)

Ierapetra (Hierapytna)

CRETA

■ **(Gortyn)**

Scale 1:3 500 000

0   80 km

0   40 miles

Mediterranean Sea

El-Arish (Rhinocolura)

4

(Paraetonium)

(Canopus)

Alexandria ■

(Sais)

(Sebennytus)

(Thmuis)

(Pelusium)

(Naucratis)

(Comarum)

(Terenuthis)

(Heliopolis)

(Clysma)

(Babylon)

Cairo

(Memphis)

QATTARA DEPRESSION

FAIYUM

(Dionysias)

(Arsinoe)

(Heracleopolis)

AEGYPTUS

ARABIAN DESERT

Gulf of Suez

3

Scale 1:4 000 000

0   200 km

0   150 miles

(Oxyrhynchuo)

Nile

Red Sea

2

El Ashmunein (Hermopolis)

(Antinoopolis)

(Antaeopolis)

El Manshah (Ptolemais Hermiou)

(Coptos)

Luxor (Thebae)

1

Isna (Latopolis)

Nile

(Apollinopolis Magna)

Kom Ombo (Ombos)

Aswan (Syene)

(Philae)

Glossary

amphitheater Really means "theater in the round" because of its oval shape. This was where gladiators fought.

amphora A huge pottery jar used to transport and store olive oil, wine, and fish sauce.

aqueduct Channel that brought water into the towns and cities, sometimes raised high upon arches to cross rivers or ravines.

barbari Literally means "barbarians." The Romans used the name for anyone who was not Roman or did not speak Latin.

basilica A long building with aisles, used as a public hall mainly for ceremonies and law courts.

censor An elected official who kept a register of all Roman citizens.

centurion A soldier in charge of about 80 to 100 men in the Roman army. His rank was similar to that of a sergeant today.

colonia A town of retired soldiers and their families set up in the provinces.

consul The highest office a politician could hold in the republic. Each year two consuls shared responsibility for the government, the army, and the law courts.

curia The name given to the building where the senate met to discuss public affairs.

diocese The name given by the emperor Diocletian to his 12 areas of government throughout the empire.

emperor *Imperator* in Latin; this was the title adopted by the emperor Augustus. An emperor held supreme power in the Roman state.

forum Originally, the open market-place in a Roman town (the Greeks called it the *agora*). Most important public buildings were grouped in and around the forum.

gladiators Warriors who fought bouts to the death in the amphitheater. They wore armor of different kinds.

hypocaust The system used to heat floors and walls of buildings, mainly the baths. Hot air from a fire flowed under raised floors and through pipes in the walls.

insula Literally means "island" and was the name for a block of buildings, surrounded by streets, in a town.

Legatus The title used by the commander of a legion and the governor of a province.

legion The main unit in the Roman army. Usually made up of about 5,500 Roman citizens in the first century C.E.

mosaic A floor (or sometimes a wall) made up of many fragments (called *tesserae*) of stone, tile, or glass. Polished smooth, it made a picture or design.

odeum A small theater used for concerts and recitals.

orator A lawyer or politician well known for making public speeches.

papyrus The Roman "paper" made from the stems of a water plant of the same name.

patricians The nobles, or upper class, of Roman society.

plebeians The name given to the ordinary working people of Roman society.

praetors The officials elected as judges in the Roman state.

procurators People appointed to look after the finances in the provinces. Some might be governors of small provinces.

provinces Areas taken over and governed by the Romans. Italy, for example, was a province of Rome.

quaestors Officials voted in to be in charge of all the state's finances —the treasury.

republic The word the Romans used for their state with its elected officials and government.

senate A large group of ex-officials who formed a type of "parliament" in Rome. They discussed public affairs and advised the elected officials such as the consuls.

thermae The Latin word for the public baths, with their sweating room (*caldarium*) and sauna (*laconicum*).

toga The outer garment (a large semicircular piece of cloth) which could only be worn by a citizen, therefore a man.

villa A farming estate as well as a house in the country or by the seaside.

FURTHER READING

Reference books about the Romans
Connolly, P. *The Cavalryman* (Oxford University Press, 1988).
Connolly, P. *The Legionary* (Oxford University Press, 1988).
Connolly, P. *The Roman Fort* (Oxford University Press, 1991).
Corbishley, M. *Illustrated Encyclopedia of Ancient Rome* (The J. Paul Getty Museum/British Museum, 2003).
Corbishley, M. *Real Romans* (English Heritage/TAG Publishing, 1999).
Corbishley, M. *The Roman World* (Watts, 1986).
Corbishley, M., and M. Cooper. *Real Romans: Digital Time Traveller* (English Heritage/TAG Publishing, 1999).
Green, M. *Roman Archaeology* (Longman, 1983).
Hodge, P. (ed.). *Roman Technology and Crafts* (Aspects of Roman Life Series, Longman, 1979).
James, S. *Ancient Rome* (Dorling Kindersley, 2004).
Macauley, D. *City: A Story of Roman Planning and Construction* (Houghton Mifflin, 1983.
Cornell, T., and J. Matthews. *Atlas of the Roman World* (Checkmark Books, 1982).
MacDonald, F. *Ancient Rome* (100 Things You Should Know About Series, Barnes & Noble, 2004).
Roberts, P. (ed.). *Ancient Rome* (Discoveries Series, Barnes & Noble, 2003).

Talbert, R. (ed.). *Atlas of Classical History* (Macmillan, 1985).

Interactive resources and Web sites
Corbishley, M., and M. Cooper. *Real Romans* (TAG/English Heritage, 1999). Text with activities, CD-ROM with games, Web sites to visit.

http://www.historyforkids.org/
Community service learning project from Portland State University.

http://www.pompeii.org
Official Web site for the state archaeological service.

http://www.silchester.rdg.ac.uk
Up-to-date information about Silchester Roman City.

http://www.romanbaths.co.uk
Web site about the Roman baths at Bath, England.

http://www.hadrians-wall.org
Web site with information and photos about this Roman frontier defense in Britian.

Gazetteer

The gazetteer lists place names found on the maps. Each place has a separate entry including a page and grid reference number. For example:
Ad Aras 57 B2

Sometimes a modern place also has an ancient name form. This name is added to the entry before the page number. For example:
Aleppo (Beroea) 87 B5

Abergavenny (Gobarrium) 67 B1
Adamclisi (Tropaeum Traiani) 75 G2
Ad Aras 57 D2
Adramyttium 80 A3
Aedepsus 77 C2
Aegae 77 C3
Aezania 80 B3
Agen (Aginnum) 61 B2
Aguntum 74 B3
Aïme (Axima) 61 C2
Aix-en-Provence (Aquae Sextiae) 61 C1
Akhisar (Thyatira) 80 B3
Alba Iulia (Apulum) 75 E3
Alcantara 56 B2
Alchester (Alauna) 67 C1
Aldborough (Isurium) 67 C3
Aleppo (Beroea) 87 B5
Alexandria 91 E4
Alexandria ad Issum 87 B5
Alfaro (Graccuris) 57 D4
Algiers (Icosium) 52 C4
Alicante (Lucentum) 57 D2
Almaden (Sisapo) 57 C2
Alvona 74 B3
Amasea 81 D4
Amastris 81 C4
Amathus 81 D1
Ambracia 77 B2
Amiens (Samarobriva) 61 B4
Amman (Philadelphia) 87 A1
Amphipolis 77 C3
Anazarbus 81 D2
Ancona 11 C4
Angers (Iuliomagus) 61 A3
Angoulême (Iculisma) 61 B2
Angustia 75 F3
Ankara (Ancyra) 81 C3
Annaba (Hippo Regius) 53 D4
Antaeopolis 91 F2
Antakya (Antiochia) 87 B5
Antalya (Attaleia) 80 C2
Antequera (Anticaria) 57 C1
Anthedon 77 C2
Antibes (Antipolis) 61 C1
Antinonopolis 87 C5
Antinoopolis 91 F2
Antiochia 80 C3
Apamea 87 B4
Aphrodisias 80 B2
Aphrodisias 75 F1
Apollinopolis Magna 91 G1
Apollonia 77 A3
Apri (Theodosiopolis) 75 G1
Aquae Regiae 53 E3
Araquil (Araceli) 57 D4
Archar (Ratiaria) 75 E2
Arezzo 11 B4
Argenton (Argentomagus) 61 B3
Argos 77 C1
Arixa (Arcobriga) 57 D3
Arles (Arelate) 61 C1
Arlon (Orolaunum) 61 C4
Arsinoe 91 F3
Ascalon 87 A2

Asine 77 C1
Asopus 77 C1
Aspendus 80 C2
Apsorus 74 B2
Astorga (Asturica Augusta) 56 B4
Aswan (Syene) 91 G1
Ataniya (Adana) 81 D2
Athens (Athenae) 77 C1
Auch (Elimberris) 61 B1
Augsburg (Augusta Vindelicorum) 74 A4
Augst (Augusta Rauricorum) 61 C3
Aureus Mons 75 D2
Autun (Augustodunum) 61 C3
Auxerre (Autessiodurum) 61 B3
Avallon (Aballo) 61 B3
Avila (Avela) 57 C3
Avranches (Legedia) 61 A4
Aydin (Tralles) 80 B2

Baalbek (Heliopolis) 87 B3
Babylon 91 F4
Baden-Baden (Aquae) 61 D4
Barca 90 A5
Barcelona (Barcino) 57 E3
Bari 11 D3
Bath (Aquae Sulis) 67 B1
Bayeux (Augustodurum) 61 A4
Bayonne (Lapurdum) 61 A1
Bazas (Vasates) 61 A2
Beauvais (Caesaromagus) 61 B4
Beersheba (Berosaba) 87 A2
Beirut (Berytus) 87 A3
Beja (Pax Iulia) 56 B2
Bejaia (Saldae) 53 D4
Belgrade (Singidunum) 11 E5, 75 D2
Benghazi (Euhesperides) 90 A5
Bergama (Pergamum) 80 B3
Bergamo 11 B5
Bergidum 56 B4
Berne 10 A6
Beroea 77 C3
Besançon (Besontio) 61 C3
Bethlehem 87 A2
Beziers (Baeterrae) 61 B1
Bilbilis 57 D3
Biskra (Vescera) 53 D3
Bistue Nova 74 C2
Bitola (Heraclea Lyncestis) 77 B3
Bitterne (Clausentum) 67 C1
Bizerte (Hippo Diarrhytus) 53 E4
Bodrum (Halicarnassus) 80 B2
Bologna 11 B5
Bonn (Bonna) 61 C5
Bordeaux (Burdigala) 61 A2
Boulogne (Gesoriacum) 61 B5
Bourges (Avaricum) 61 B3
Bowes (Lavatrae) 67 B3
Bowness (Maia) 66 E5, 67 B3
Braga (Bracara Augusto) 56 B3
Brancaster (Branodunum) 67 D2
Bregenz (Brigantium) 74 A3
Brescia 11 B5
Bressuire (Segora) 61 A3
Brindisi 11 D3
Brough (Petuaria) 67 C2
Brough (Verterae) 67 B3
Brza Palanka (Egeta) 75 E2
Bubon 80 B2
Budapest (Aquincum) 74 D3
Burnam 74 C2
Bursa (Prusa) 80 B4
Buseire (Circesium) 87 D4
Busra (Bostra) 87 B3
Buxton (Aquae Arnemetiae) 67 C2

Cabeza de Griego (Segobriga) 57 D2

Caceres (Norba) 56 B2
Cadiz (Gadez) 56 B1
Caeleon (Isca) 67 B1
Caernarvon (Segontium) 67 A2
Caerwent (Venta) 67 B1
Caesarea Maritima 87 A3
Caesarea Paneas 87 A3
Cagliari 11 B2
Cahors (Divona) 61 B2
Cairo 91 F3
Caister (Venta) 67 D2
Calahorra (Calagurris) 57 D4
Cambrai (Camaracum) 61 B5
Cambridge (Durolipons) 67 D2
Canopus 91 F4
Canterbury (Durovernum) 67 D1
Carcassonne (Carcaso) 61 B1
Carlisle (Luguvalium) 66 F5, 67 B3
Carmarthen (Moridunum) 67 A1
Carnutum 74 C4
Carpasia 81 D1
Cartagena (Carthago Nova) 57 D1
Carvoran (Magnis) 66 F5
Casablanca 52 A2
Casei (Samum) 75 E3
Castel Roussilion (Ruscino) 61 B1
Castlesteads 66 F5
Castra Traiana 75 F3
Catania 11 D1
Catterick (Cataractonium) 67 C3
Celei (Sucidava) 75 F2
Celje (Celcia) 74 C3
Chalon-sur-Saône (Cavillonum) 61 C3
Chartres (Autricum) 61 B4
Chelmsford (Caesaromagus) 67 D1
Cherbourg (Coriallum) 61 A4
Cherchell (Iol Caesarea) 52 C4
Chersonesus 91 I6
Chester (Deva) 67 B2
Chesterholm (Vindolanda) 66 F5
Chesters (Cilurnum) 66 F6
Chichester (Noviomagus) 67 C1
Cimiez (Cemenelum) 61 C1
Cirencester (Corinium) 67 C1
Cissa 74 C2
Claudiopolis 81 C4
Claudiopolis 81 D2
Clermont-Ferrand (Augustonemetum) 61 B2
Clysma 91 G4
Cohors Breucorum 52 C3
Coimbra (Aeminium) 56 B3
Colchester (Camulodunum) 67 D1
Comama 80 C2
Comana Pontica 81 E4
Comarum 91 E4
Constantine (Cirta) 53 D4
Coptos 91 G2
Corbridge (Corstopitum) 66 F5, 67 B3
Cordoba (Corduba) 57 C1
Corfu (Corcyra) 77 A2
Corinium 74 C2
Corinth (Corinthus) 77 C1
Cucusus 81 E3
Cumidava 75 F3
Cuprija (Horreum Margi) 75 E2
Curicum 74 B3
Curium 81 C1
Cyaneae 80 B2
Cyme 80 A3
Cyrrhus 87 B5
Cyzicus 80 B4

Damascus 87 B3
Danaba 87 B4
Decize (Decetia) 61 B3
Delminium 74 C2
Delphi 77 C2
Demetrias 77 C2
Denia (Dianium) 57 E2
Derna (Darnis) 90 B5
Deultum 75 G2
Diana Veteranorum 53 D3
Digne (Dinia) 61 C2
Dijon (Diblo) 61 C3
Dinar (Celaenae) 80 C3
Dionysias 91 F3
Diospolis 87 A2
Dium 77 C3
Djemila (Cuicul) 53 D4
Dodona 77 B2
Dorchester (Durnovaria) 67 B1
Dorchester (Durnovaria) 67 C1
Doriscus 75 F1
Dougga (Thugga) 53 E4
Dover (Dubris) 67 D1
Droitwich (Salinae) 67 B2
Drumburgh (Congavata) 66 E5
Dunakömlöd (Lussonium) 74 D3
Dura-Europus 87 D4
Durostorum 75 D2
Durrës (Epidamnus) 77 A3

Ebchester (Vindomora) 67 G5
Ecija (Astigi) 57 C1
Edirne (Hadrianopolis) 75 F1, 52 C1
Elaeusa 81 D2
El-Arish (Rhinocolura) 91 G4
El Ashmunein (Hermopolis Magna) 91 F2
El Asnam (Castellum Tingitanum) Elat (Aila) 87 A2
Eleusis 77 C2
El Jem (Thysdrus) 53 E3
El Kantara (Calceus Herculis) 53 D3
El Kef (Sicca Veneria) 53 E4
El Manshah (Ptolemais Hermiou) 91 F2
el Padron (Iria Elavia) 56 B4
El Qanawat (Canatha) 87 B3
Embrun (Eburodurum) 61 C2
Epfach (Abudiacum) 74 A3
Ephesus 80 B2
Eregli (Heraclea Pontica) 81 C4
Erythrae 80 A3
Eskishehir (Dorylaeum) 80 C3
Estrées-sur-Noye 61 B4
Eupatoria 81 E4
Evora (Ebora) 56 B2
Exeter (Isca) 67 B1

Faro (Ossonoba) 56 B1
Ferrara 11 B5
Fès 52 A3
Feurs (Forum Segusiavorcum) 61 C2
Fishbourne 67 C1
Florence 11 B4
Foggia 11 D3
Forlì 11 C5
Fréjus (Forum Iulii) 61 C1

Gabès (Tacapae) 53 E2
Gafsa (Capsa) 53 E3
Gangra 81 D4
Garsaura 81 D3
Gaza 87 A2
Gazipasa (Selinus) 81 C2
Geneva 61 C3
Genoa 11 A5
Geraestus 77 D1

Gerona (Gerunda) 57 E3
Gibraltar (Calpe) 57 C1
Gijon (Gigia) 57 C4
Gloucester (Glevum) 67 B1
Godmanchester (Durovigutum) 67 C2
Gorsium 74 D3
Gortyn 91 I6
Grenoble (Cularo) 61 C2
Györ (Arrabona) 74 C3
Guadix (Acci) 57 C1
Gunzburg (Guntia) 74 A4

Haidra (Ammaedara) 53 E3
Halae 77 C2
Halton (Onnum) 66 G6
Hama (Epiphania) 87 B4
Harran (Carrhae) 87 C5
Hebron 87 A2
Hedum 74 D2
Heliopolis 91 F4
Hephaestia 77 D2
Heracleia 75 G2
Heracleopolis 91 F3
Herodion 87 A2
High Rochester (Bremenium) 67 B3
Homs (Emesa) 87 B4
Housesteads (Vercovicium) 66 F6
Huercal (Urci) 57 D1
Huesca (Osca) 57 D4

Iader 74 C2
Ierapetra (Hierapytna) 91 J6
Ilchester (Lindinis) 67 B1
Inchtuthil (Victoria) 67 B3
Inebolu (Abonuteichus) 81 D4
Innsbruk (Veldidena) 74 A3
Inveresk (Coria) 67 B3
Isaura 81 C2
Isna (Latopolis) 91 G1
Issus 81 E2
Istanbul (Byzantium) 75 G1
Isthmia 77 C1
Italica 56 B1
Itanus 91 J6
Izmir (Smyrna) 80 B3
Izmit (Nicomedia) 80 B4
Iznik (Nicaea) 80 B4

Jarash (Gerasa) 87 A3
Jericho 87 A1
Jerusalem (Aelia Capitolina) 87 A2
Jijel (Igilgili) 53 D4

Kadiköy (Chalcedon) 80 B4
Kaliste (Municipium) 75 E2
Karaman (Laranda) 81 D2
Karnak (Characmoba) 87 A2
Karpuzu (Alinda) 80 B2
Kastelli (Cisamum) 91 H6
Kavalla (Neapolis) 77 D3
Kayseri (Mazaca) 81 D3
Kenchela (Mascula) 53 D3
Kenchester (Magnis) 67 B2
Khamissa (Thubursicu Numidarum) 53 D4
Khania (Cydonia) 91 I6
Koblenz (Confluentes) 61 C5
Köln (Colonia Agrippina) 61 C5
Kom Ombo (Ombos) 91 G1
Komotini (Porsule) 75 F1
Konstanz (Constantia) 74 A3
Konya (Iconium) 81 C2
Kostolac (Viminacium) 75 E2

La Coruna (Brigantium) 56 B4
Lambese (Lambaesis) 53 D3
Laodicea 87 A4

93

Lapithos (Lapethus) 81 D1
Lapseki (Lampsacus) 80 A4
Larisa 77 C2
Larnaca (Citium) 81 D1
La Spezia 11 B5
Lectoure (Lactora) 61 B1
Leicester (Ratae) 67 C2
Leiva (Libia) 57 C4
Lejjun 87 A3
Le Mans (Suindinum) 61 B3
Léon (Legio) 57 C4
Leptis Magna 53 F2
Lerida (Ilerda) 57 E3
Levadhia (Lebadea) 77 C2
Lezuza (Libisosa) 57 D2
Limenia 81 C1
Limoges (Augustoritum) 61 B2
Lincoln (Lindum) 67 C2
Lind (Ad Pontem) 74 B3
Lisbon (Olisipo) 56 A2
Lisieux (Noviomagus) 61 B4
Lissus 75 D1
Littlechester (Derventio) 67 C2
Lixus 52 A3
Ljubljana 11 C6
Lodève (Luteva) 61 B1
London (Londinium) 67 C1
Lorch (Lauriacum) 74 B4
Lovech (Melta) 75 F2
Lugo (Lucus Augusti) 56 B4
Luxor (Thebae) 91 G1
Lyon (Lugdunum) 61 C2

Madaba 87 A2
Madrid 57 C3
Magnum 74 C2
Mahón (Mago) 57 E2
Maienfeld (Magia) 74 A3
Mainz (Moguntiacum) 61 D5
Malaga (Malaca) 57 C1
Malatya (Melitene) 81 E3
Maluesa 75 D2
Manchester (Mamucium) 67 B2
Mangalia (Callatis) 75 G2
Mantinea 77 C1
Marathon 77 C2
Marcianopolis 75 G2
Marrakech 52 A1
Marsa Susah (Apollonia) 90 A5
Marseille (Massilia) 61 C1
Martos (Tucci) 57 C1
Masada 87 A2
Mautern (Faviana) 74 C4
Medellin (Metellinum) 56 C2
Megalopolis 77 C1
Mehadia (Ad Mediam) 75 E2
Melilla (Rusaddir) 52 B3
Membij (Hierapolis) 87 B5
Memphis 91 F3
Merida (Emerita Augusta) 56 B2
Mertola (Myrtilis) 56 B1
Mesa de Asta (Hasta) 56 B1
Messad (Castellum Dimmidi) 52 C3
Messina 11 D2
Messini (Messene) 77 B1
Metropolis 77 B2
Metz (Divodurum) 61 C4
Milan 11 B5
Mitrovica (Sirmium) 75 D2
Moigrad (Porolissum) 75 E3
Montana 75 E2
Montoro (Epora) 57 C2
Mostaganem 52 C3
Moutiers (Darantasia) 61 C2
Mycenae 77 C1
Myra 80 B2
Mytilene 80 A3

Nabeul (Neapolis) 53 E4
Nantes (Portus Namnetum) 61 A3
Naples 11 C3
Narbonne (Narbo) 61 B1
Narona 74 C2
Naryca 77 C2
Naucratis 91 F4
Naupactus 77 B2
Naxos 77 D1
Nazareth 87 A3
Neapolis 87 A3
Nefta (Nepete) 53 E2
Néris-les-Bains (Aquae Neri) 61 B3
Nesebur (Mesembria) 75 G2
Nessana 87 A2
Netherby (Castra Exploratorum) 66 F6, 67 B3
Neuburg (Submuntorium) 74 A4
Neuss (Novaesium) 61 C5
Newcastle (Pons Aelius) 67 C3, 67 G5
Newstead (Trimontium) 67 B3
Nicopolis 77 B2
Nicopolis 81 E4
Nicopolis ad Istrum 75 F2
Nicopolis ad Nestum 75 E1
Nijmegen (Noviomagus) 61 C5
Nijon (Noviomagus) 61 C4
Nîmes (Nemausus) 61 C1
Nis (Naissus) 75 E2
Nizy (Minatiacum) 61 C4
Novae 75 F2
Nusaybin (Nisibis) 87 D5
Nyons (Noviodunum) 61 C3

Oboda 87 A2
Oenoanda 80 B2
Oescus 75 F2
Ohrid (Lychnidus) 77 A3
Olbasa 80 B2
Old Sarum (Sorviodunum) 67 C1
Olympia 77 B1
Oporto (Oportus Cale) 56 B3
Oppidum Novum 52 A3
Oran (Portus Magnus) 52 B3
Orange (Arausio) 61 C2
Oretum 57 C2
Oricum 77 A3
Osijek (Mursa) 74 D3
Osma (Uxama Argela) 57 C3
Osuna (Urso) 57 C1
Oudna (Uthina) 53 E4
Oviedo (Ovetum) 57 C4
Oxyrhynchus 91 F3

Padua 11 B5
Palanka (Lederata) 75 E2
Palencia (Pallantia) 57 C4
Palermo 11 C2
Palma 57 E2
Palmyra 87 C4
Pamplona (Pompaelo) 57 D4
Pamukkale (Hierapolis) 80 B2
Paphus 81 C1
Paraetonium 91 D4
Paris (Lutetia) 61 B4
Parma 11 B5
Passau (Castra Batava) 74 B4
Passau-Instadt (Boiodurum) 74 B4
Patras (Patrae) 77 B2
Pecs (Sopianae) 74 D3
Pella 77 C3
Pelusium 91 G4
Périgueux (Vesunna) 61 B2
Perinthus 75 G1
Perugia 11 C4

Pescara 11 C4
Pessinus 81 C3
Petra 87 A2
Pevensey (Anderita) 67 D1
Philae 91 G1
Philippi 77 D3
Philippopolis (Plovdiv) 75 F2
Phoenix 91 I6
Piacenza 11 B5
Piraeus 77 C1
Pisa 11 B4
Podandus 81 D2
Poitiers (Limonum) 61 B3
Pollensa (Pollentia) 57 E2
Pons Aluti 75 F2
Portus Victoriae 57 C4
Potidaea 77 C3
Praetorium 75 F3
Priene 80 B2
Ptuj (Poetovio) 74 C3

Qirzah (Ghirza) 53 F1

Rabat 52 A3
Raqqa (Nic Horium) 87 C4
Raphanaea 87 B4
Ravenna 11 C5
Regensburg (Castra Regina) 74 B4
Reggio di Calabria 11 D2
Reims (Durocortorum) 61 C4
Rennes (Condate) 61 A4
Retortillo (Iuliobriga) 57 C4
Rhodes (Rhodus) 80 B2
Rhodiapolis 80 C2
Ribchester (Bremetennacum) 67 B2
Richborough (Rutupiae) 67 D1
Rimini 11 C5
Risafe (Resapha) 87 C4
Risinium 74 D2
Rochester (Durobrivae) 67 D1
Rochester (Vindovala) 67 G6
Rodez (Segodunum) 61 B2
Rom (Rauranum) 61 B3
Rome 11 C3
Rosenheim (Pons Aeni) 74 B3
Rouen (Rotomagus) 61 B4
Royan (Noviorigum) 61 A2
Rusucurru 53 C4

Sadouri (Ausum) 53 D3
Sagalassus 80 B2
Saguntum 57 D2
Saida (Sidon) 87 A3
St. Albans (Verulamium) 67 C1
St. Rémy (Glanum) 61 C1
Sais 91 F4
Salamanca (Salmantica) 57 C3
Salamis 81 D1
Salerno 11 C3
Salonae 74 C2
Saloniki (Thessalonica) 77 C3
Salvium 74 C2
Salzburg (Iuvavum) 74 B3
Sami (Same) 77 B2
Samothracia 77 D3
Samsat (Samosata) 87 C5
Samsun (Amisus) 81 E4
Santarem (Scallabis) 56 B2
Sarajevo 11 E4
Sarande (Onchesmus) 77 B2
Sardis 80 B3
Sarduc (Centum Putei) 75 E3
Sarmizegetusa 75 E3
Sasamon (Segisamo) 57 C4
Sassari 11 A3
Satala 81 F4
Sbeitla (Sufetula) 53 E3

Scardonia 74 C2
Scitarijevo (Andautonia) 74 C3
Scodra 75 D2
Scythopolis 87 A3
Sebennytus 91 F4
Sées (Seii) 61 B4
Segovia 57 C3
Selge 80 C2
Selimiye (Side) 81 C2
Senia 74 B3
Sens (Agedincum) 61 B4
Seriane 87 B4
Setif (Sitifis) 53 D4
Seville (Hispalis) 56 B1
Sfax (Taparura) 53 E3
Shahhat (Cyrene) 90 A5
Sicyon 77 C1
Side 81 E4
Siga 52 B3
Sigacik (Teos) 80 A3
Silchester (Calleva) 67 C1
Silifke (Seleucia) 81 D2
Simancas (Septimanca) 57 C3
Singara 87 D5
Sinop (Sinope) 81 D5
Sisak (Siscia) 74 C3
Sivas (Megalopolis) 81 E3
Skopje (Scupi) 75 E2
Sofia (Serdica) 75 E2
Soli 81 D2
Sousse (Hadrumetum) 53 E3
South Shields 67 G5
Sparti (Sparta) 77 C1
Speyer (Noviomagus) 61 D4
Split (Aspalathos) 74 C2
Stanwix 66 F5
Stara Zagora (Beroe) 75 F2
Stobi 77 B3
Strasbourg (Argentorate) 61 C4
Stratus 77 B2
Susa (Segusio) 61 C2
Synnada 80 C3
Szombathely (Savaria) 74 C3
Szöny (Brigetio) 74 D3

Tabarka (Thabraca) 53 E4
Tadcaster (Calcaria) 67 C2
Talavera la Vieja (Augustobriga) 57 C2
Tamassus 81 D1
Tangiers (Tingi) 52 A3
Taranto 11 D3
Tarazona (Turiasso) 57 D3
Tarragona (Tarraco) 57 E3
Tarsatica 74 B3
Tarsus 81 D2
Tavium 81 D3
Tebessa (Thevestis) 53 E3
Tel Aviv-Yafo (Joppa) 87 A3
Telmessus 80 B2
Telmine (Turris Tamallent) 53 E2
Ténès (Cartenna) 52 C4
Terenuthis 91 F4
Terni 11 C4
Teturnia 74 B3
Teuthrone 77 C1
Thamusida 52 A3
Thapsus 53 E3
Thasos 77 D3
Thebes (Thebae) 77 C2
Thera 77 D1
Thisvi (Thisbe) 77 C2
Thmuis 91 F4
Tiberias 87 A3
Tiklat (Tupusuctu) 53 D4
Timgad (Thamugadi) 53 D3
Tinos 77 D1
Tiranë 11 E3
Titulcia 57 C3

Tlemcen (Pomaria) 52 B3
Toledo (Toletum) 57 C2
Tongeren (Atuatuca) 61 C5
Tortosa (Dertosa) 57 E3
Toul (Tullum) 61 C4
Toulouse (Tolosa) 61 B1
Tournai (Turnacum) 61 B5
Tours (Caesarodunum) 61 B3
Towcester (Lactodorum) 67 C2
Trapezus 81 F4
Trier (Augusta Treverorum) 61 C4
Trieste 11 C5
Trikkala (Tricca) 77 B2
Tripoli (Oea) 53 F2
Tripoli (Tripolis) 87 A4
Troesmis 75 G3
Troezen 77 C1
Trogir (Tragurium) 74 C2
Troy (Ilium) 80 A3
Troyes (Augustobona) 61 C4
Tukrah (Tauchira) 90 A5
Tulln (Commagena) 74 C4
Tulmaythah (Ptolemais) 90 A5
Tunis (Carthago) 11 B1, 53 E4
Turin 10 A5
Turnu-Severin (Drobeta) 75 E2
Tyana 81 D2
Tyre (Tyrus) 87 A3

Ulmetum 75 G2
Ulpia Traiana Sarmizegetusa 75 E3
Ulpianum 75 E2
Um Qeis (Gadara) 87 A3
Urfa (Edessa) 87 C5
Utique (Utica) 53 E4
Uzès (Ucetia) 61 C2

Valencia (Valentia) 57 D2
Valkenburg 61 C6
Varna (Odessus) 75 G2
Venice 11 C5
Verona 11 B5
Vevey (Viviscus) 61 C3
Vicenza 11 B5
Vich (Ausa) 57 E3
Vienna (Vindobona) 74 C4
Vienne (Vienna) 61 C2
Villach (Santicum) 74 B3
Vinkovci (Cibalae) 74 D3
Virunum 74 B3
Vize (Bizye) 75 F1

Wallsend (Segedunum) 67 C3, 67 G5
Water Newton (Durobrivae) 67 C2
Weisbaden (Aquae Mattiacae) 61 D5
Wels (Ovilava) 74 B4
Willoughby (Vernemetum) 67 C2
Winchester (Venta) 67 C1
Windisch (Vindonissa) 61 D3
Worms (Borbetomagus) 61 D4
Wroxeter (Viroconium) 67 B2

Xanten (Vetera) 61 C5
Xanthus 80 B2

York (Eburacum) 67 C2

Zagreb 11 D5
Zamora (Ocelum Duri) 57 C3
Zaragoza (Caesaraugusta) 57 D3
Zeugma 87 B5
Zintan (Tentheos) 53 F2
Zuccabar 52 A3

Index